BILLIARD PRACTICE DRILLS
CONTAINING:

ELEMENTRY: ONE BALL PRACTICE,
MOTION, IMPACT AND DIVISION OF BALLS:
TWO BALL PRACTICE AND PLAIN STROKES, WINNING
AND LOSING HAZARDS, CANNONS: THREE BALL PRACTICE

BY

W. BROADFOOT

Copyright © 2013 Read Books Ltd.
This book is copyright and may not be
reproduced or copied in any way without
the express permission of the publisher in writing

British Library Cataloguing-in-Publication Data
A catalogue record for this book is available from the
British Library

Billiards, Pool and Snooker

Cue sports, also known as billiard sports, are a wide variety of games of skill, generally played with a cue stick, used to strike billiard balls, moving them around a cloth-covered billiards table bounded by rubber cushions. Historically, the umbrella term was billiards. While that familiar name is still employed by some as a generic label for all such games, the word's usage has splintered into more exclusive competing meanings in various parts of the world. For example, in British and Australian English, 'billiards' usually refers exclusively to the game of English billiards, while in American and Canadian English, it is sometimes used to refer to a particular game or class of games, or to all cue games in general, depending upon dialect and context. The World Professional Billiards and Snooker Association (WPBSA) was established in 1968 to regulate the professional game, while the International Billiards and Snooker Federation (IBSF) regulates the amateur games.

There are three major subdivisions of games within cue sports: 'Carom billiards', referring to games played on tables without pockets, typically 10 feet in length, including balkline and straight rail, cushion caroms, three-cushion billiards, artistic billiards and four-ball. 'Pool', covering numerous pocket billiards games generally played on six-pocket tables of 7-, 8-, or 9-foot length, including among others eight-ball (the world's most widely played cue sport), nine-ball, ten-ball, straight pool, one-pocket and bank pool. And 'Snooker / English Billiards'; games played on a billiards table with six pockets called a snooker table (which has dimensions just under 12 ft by 6 ft). Such games are classified entirely separately from pool, based on a separate historical development, as well as a separate culture and terminology that characterize their play. More obscurely, there are games that make use of obstacles and targets, and table-top games played with disks instead of balls.

Billiards has a long and rich history stretching from its inception in the fifteenth century. Legendarily, Mary Queen of Scots was buried wrapped in her much loved billiard table cover in 1586. The sport has been mentioned many times in the works of Shakespeare, including the famous line 'let's to billiards' in *Antony and Cleopatra* (1606-7). There have also been many famous enthusiasts of the sport, including Mozart, Louis XIV of France, Marie Antoinette, Immanuel Kant, Napoleon, Abraham Lincoln and Mark Twain. All cue sports are generally regarded to have evolved into indoor games from outdoor stick-and-ball lawn games (retroactively termed ground billiards), and as such to be related to trucco, croquet and golf, and more distantly to the stickless bocce and balls. The word 'billiard' may have evolved from the French word *billart* or *billette*, meaning 'stick', and a recognizable form of billiards was played outdoors in the 1340s, reminiscent of croquet.

King Louis XI of France (1461–1483) had the first known indoor billiard table, and having further refined and popularised the game, it swiftly spread amongst the French nobility. Early billiard games involved various pieces of additional equipment, including the 'arch' (related to the croquet hoop), 'port' (a different hoop) and 'king' (a pin or skittle near the arch) in the 1770s. However other game variants, relying on the cushions (and eventually on pockets cut into them), were being formed that would go on to play fundamental roles in the development of modern billiards. The early croquet-like games eventually led to the development of the carom or carambole billiards category, what most non-Commonwealth and non-US speakers today mean by the word 'billiards'. These games, which once completely dominated the cue sports world have declined markedly over the last few generations. They were traditionally played with three or sometimes four balls, on a table without holes (and without obstructions or targets in most cases), in which the goal is generally to strike one object ball with a cue ball, then have the cue ball rebound off of one or more of the cushions and strike a second object ball.

Over time, a type of obstacle returned, originally as a hazard and later as a target, in the form of pockets, or holes partly cut into the table bed and partly into the cushions, leading to the rise of pocket billiards, including 'pool' games such as eight-ball, nine-ball and snooker. Today, there are many variations of 'billiards' including Straightline rail, Balkline and Three-chsion billiards.

Two-player or team-games such as 'Eight-ball', where the goal is to pocket all of one's designated group of balls (either stripes vs. solids, or reds vs. yellows, depending upon the equipment), and then pocket the 8 ball in a called pocket, or 'Nine-ball', where the goal is to pocket the 9 ball, through hitting (each time) the lowest-numbered object ball remaining on the table – have become very popular. 'Snooker' is largely played in the United Kingdom; by far the most common cue sport at competitive level, and a major national pastime. It is played in many other countries, although is unpopular in America, where eight-ball and nine-ball dominate, and Latin-America where carom games dominate. The first International Snooker Championship was held in 1927, and it has been held annually since then with few exceptions.

ELEMENTARY : ONE-BALL PRACTICE

BEFORE commencing the manual of instruction in billiards, it is desirable to address a few words of advice to the beginner, and to explain some of the technical terms used. Others will be described in future chapters.

It is clear that before playing, the room must be entered ; and hence we commence with the mode of doing so. The operation seems so simple as to be too trivial for notice ; but, far from that, there is nothing short of actual play which shows more clearly the difference between a well-trained, well-mannered player and a novice or a careless and discourteous visitor. The door of a room should always be approached quietly, for the table may be occupied ; if it be so, *wait for the stroke.* When the stroke is played, open the door quietly, and walk straight to a seat. Avoid everything likely to distract the attention of the players from their game, and recollect that for the time being the room, its light, fire, and so forth, belong to them. Persons who smoke should wait for the stroke before scratching a match, and when extinguishing it should not do so by waving it before the eyes of the player. In short, ordinary courtesy is nowhere more important than in the billiard-room, for if men can play, their nerve and attention are strained ; interruption may prove fatal to the chance of one of them, and is sure to be resented, even though it may pass without remark.

In the previous chapter the terms employed respecting the

PRELIMINARIES.

ELEMENTARY: ONE-BALL PRACTICE

table and implements have been detailed; these are now supplemented by others in common use during play.

Angled.—A ball is angled in respect to that part of the table to which it cannot be directly played.

Ball.—In billiards three balls are used, white, spot-white, and red. The player's or cue-ball will usually, in this volume, be called ball 1; the object ball, or ball played on, ball 2; and the third ball, ball 3. A line-ball is one resting on the baulk-line.

Baulk.—The space between the baulk-line and the bottom cushion. A ball within that space is in *baulk*; when a white and red ball are in baulk and the other is off the table, the situation is termed a *double-baulk*.

Break.—The term is applied to a continuous score, or one made in unbroken succession.

To *break the balls* is to play as at the opening of a game.

Bridge.—The player's hand which rests on the table, and which serves as a guide to the cue, is so called.

Coup.—If a player fails to hit another ball, and by the same stroke causes his own ball to enter a pocket, he is said to have *run a coup*.

Cover.—A ball is said to be *covered* when it cannot be directly hit by player's ball because of the interposition of another ball; in other words, when ball 1 cannot directly strike ball 2 because of ball 3, ball 2 is said to be *covered* by ball 3.

Foul.—A stroke made in contravention of the rules.

In hand.—When a player's ball is off the table it is termed *in hand*.

Hazard.—When a player with his ball pockets another ball he is said to make a *winning hazard*; when he pockets his own ball after contact with another ball he makes a *losing hazard*.

Kiss.—Ball 2 is said to kiss when it comes a second time in contact with ball 1. The kiss is generally made off a cushion.

This term is used with much laxity in the language of billiards, and includes what the French call *coups durs*, when ball 2 is touching a cushion, and *rencontres*, when balls 1 and 3 meet, the former having been set in motion by the cue and the latter by the impact of ball 2. When ball 2 has an unforeseen collision with ball 3, and thereby prevents a cannon, the failure is attributed to robbery by a *kiss*.

Miss-cue.—Failure in the delivery of the cue on player's ball; usually a slip from want of chalk or from defective striking.

Plant.—When two balls touch and an imaginary line through their centres if prolonged terminates in the centre of a pocket, a *dead plant* is said to be on. If the ball further from the pocket be played on and struck almost anywhere, the ball nearer the pocket will inevitably be *planted* or go into the pocket. The *plant* is still possible when the line through the centres falls slightly to the right or left of the pocket.

Strength is the measure of force used to make a stroke, which is said to be soft or hard according to the *strength*.

Stringing

To *string* is to play from baulk to the top cushion so as to leave player's ball near the baulk-line or bottom cushion as may be selected. Before a match the players *string* simul-

ELEMENTARY: ONE-BALL PRACTICE

taneously for choice of balls, and for the option of commencing the game.

After these preliminaries, the first matter of importance is that players should try to acquire an easy attitude. For its attainment precise rules like those for military drill cannot be given, because what are suitable for a tall spare man are wholly impossible to one who is short and stout.

An Easy Attitude

Therefore, advice must be general. The learner should go to a proficient of about his own make, whose style is admitted to be good, and be shown the best attitudes to reach a ball placed in various parts of the table, first from baulk, and afterwards from other and more cramped positions. If this be neglected, he is apt to contract faulty habits, which become more difficult to abandon the longer they have been entertained.

In playing an ordinary stroke from baulk, a right-handed player should stand so that his body shall be on the left of the line of stroke, which is, in fact, the axis of the cue; the left foot should be advanced so that the toe shall be just below the cushion, and pointing in the direction of the stroke; the right foot retired more or less according to the stature of the player, and pointing at a right angle to the left foot. The right leg should be straight, the left more or less bent; the right hand should hold the cue near the butt, the elbow being nearly vertically above the hand, whilst the left hand should be extended in the line of stroke, so that the cue resting between the thumb and forefinger shall lie as nearly as possible horizontal. For a left-handed player the same advice holds good, save that throughout the word 'left' should be substituted for 'right.' For all players that attitude is best which is least stiff or constrained, and which combines the greatest measure of steadiness with freedom of action.

The formation of a good bridge is essential to accurate play. Its object is to supply a rest for the cue at the height of the stroke to be delivered, and this ordinarily is the centre of the ball. Just as for the right hand, which puts the cue in motion, freedom is the chief necessity, so for the left, which acts as the guide and support, stability is of the first importance. That is best attained by bringing some weight to bear on the base of the thumb, and consequently by somewhat raising the knuckle-joint of the little finger. As hands vary in shape and size, no precise rule or measurements for the formation of a bridge can be laid down. A competent instructor will show how a bridge is made, and an intelligent learner will soon acquire the habit of making one which suits himself. The general mode is to place the hand flat on the table, elevate the knuckles about two inches or rather more, keeping the fingers rigid or unbent, so as to form nearly a right angle with the palm, raise the thumb, and press it moderately just above the joint against the forefinger, forming with it the rest or point of support of the cue, spread the fingers slightly so as to widen the foundation, so to speak, of the bridge and increase its stability, and by means of raising or lowering the little finger, bring the point of support so that the cue shall lie level with the point of the ball to be struck. These directions, perhaps, seem complicated; but if the pre-

ELEMENTARY: ONE-BALL PRACTICE

scribed movements are gone through once or twice before the learner by a competent person, all difficulty will disappear. The final movement whereby the height of delivery of the cue is regulated, is one of much importance, which we do not recollect to have seen mentioned in previous manuals.

Exceptional rests or bridges have to be made to meet exceptional cases. Thus, when a ball is under a cushion, the tips of the fingers form the sole support; in other instances

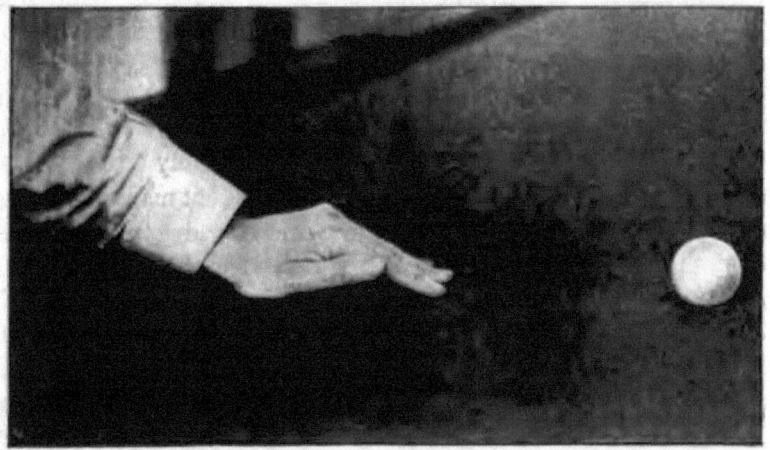

The Bridge

the thumb is lowered and the forefinger bent so as to form a ring or hook through which the cue is passed. The French call this *bouclée*.[1] There are, in fact, many variations which it would be a waste of time and space to describe; some, indeed, have to be invented as the necessity for their use may arise.

The attitude and method of making a bridge having been acquired, the next point is to deliver the cue freely and horizontally. It should be lightly held near the butt and repose on the bridge, so that ordinarily from 9 to 12 inches project towards the ball. Considerable differences in the distances between the bridge and the ball occur during the variations in a game, but it is generally

[1] See illustration, p. 129.

true that the nearer they are the greater the accuracy with which the ball can be struck, and the further (within reasonable limits) they are apart the greater the power. What is gained in power is, to some extent, lost in accuracy.

A little practice with the cue without a ball is useful to familiarise a beginner with the necessary action, that is the horizontal backward and forward motion; a slow withdrawal followed by a faster forward stroke. When this is attained practice with one ball should be commenced. It is of the highest importance; for by means of it alone can the rare qualification of a true delivery of cue be acquired. And this applies not merely to beginners, but to persons who are out of practice, for the commonest of all faults, and the secret of most failures to score, is that the player's ball is not truly struck. It may seem strange, but it is nevertheless true, that many persons who play what is held to be a fair game cannot truly strike a ball.

Let us then suppose a ball placed on the spot on the centre of the baulk circle, and that the player has assumed a suitable attitude in order to play up the table over the billiard spot. The tip of his cue should be about half an inch from the centre of the ball, and the axis of the cue should be as nearly as possible parallel with the surface of the table, and in the same vertical plane as its central line, because the path travelled by a ball truly struck in the centre is, till after impact with a cushion or with another ball, invariably a prolongation of the axis of the cue. Having aimed carefully over the spot, he should draw the cue slowly back three or four inches and then bring it forward, giving the ball a smart tap, in contradistinction to a push, in the centre; the strength of the stroke to be such that the ball shall return into baulk. If ball, table, and stroke are true, the path travelled will lie precisely over all the spots in the central line; and after impact with the top cushion the ball will return to baulk by the same route. Herein is manifest the excellence of this stroke for practice; because if the ball be struck either right or left of the centre, it will return to the right or left of the central longitudinal line of the table. The nearer

ELEMENTARY: ONE-BALL PRACTICE

the return path is to that line the better the stroke, and the further it is from it the worse ; so that an infallible measure of the truth or accuracy of hitting the ball is supplied by the result. It is impossible to overstate the value of this test, and by the time that a person can play this stroke up and down the table with varying strength and fair accuracy he has gone far towards mastering the first step at billiards. To secure striking the ball in the centre, as soon as aim is taken the player should fix his eyes on the ball and try to the best of his ability to deliver the cue truly and as horizontally as possible so that the tip does not see-saw up and down. The tap on the centre of the ball should be sharp and clean, the cue being permitted to follow it for a few inches ; less when the stroke is soft, and more when it is hard.

It may probably appear in course of practice that the striker has a tendency to hit the ball either right or left of the centre ; he should correct this by striking on what seems to him slightly the other side. Thus, if he, whilst aiming truly, brings the ball back to baulk invariably to the right of the central line, he should strike at what seems to him slightly to the *left* of its centre ; if by doing so he brings the ball back over the spots, he may be assured that he has found the true centre of the ball, and by continuing the practice his eye will become educated, and the tendency to strike on the side will diminish or disappear. The stroke should be repeated till it is mastered at every possible strength, or, say, hard enough to cause the ball to travel four lengths of the table. When confidence in 'the power to strike a ball in the centre has been acquired, further practice should be made. Place the ball on one corner spot of the **D**, play to the centre of the top cushion immediately behind the spot, and the ball should return over the spot on the other corner. This, too, is very useful practice ; it familiarises the eye with the general truth of the axiom that the angle of reflexion is equal to the angle of incidence ; and variations from this stroke (which need not be defined here, as any person of ordinary intelligence can multiply them indefinitely) will prove of constant use when it is necessary to play at a ball protected by baulk.

For the sake of clearness, one other example may be cited.

Place the ball on the right corner of the **D**, measure a point on the top cushion an equal distance from the right side cushion, that point will be precisely opposite the right corner of the **D**; halve the distance between that point and the left top pocket, and at the half set up a mark—a piece of chalk laid on the cushion will do. If the ball be played correctly on to the place thus indicated, it will return to the left bottom pocket. Easier strokes of the same kind can be made across the table into any pocket, and confidence, which is an important factor in the game, is thus acquired. Before leaving the subject of these exercise strokes, it is desirable to emphasise the value to a beginner of acquiring a good style and of cultivating it incessantly till it becomes natural, and then he may, without harm, indulge occasionally in a game; if he begins with games he is certain to contract bad habits, which, becoming more confirmed the longer he plays, must result in increasing his difficulties and may never be wholly cured.

As regards indicating the strength to be used in playing various strokes, the best plan is to refer to the positions of the balls when they are at rest after a stroke; but as some rough guide may save beginners many trials, it has been usual to indicate by means of numbers the approximate strength to be used. Thus Strength No. 1 is a slow, or soft stroke; No. 2 harder, and so on till No. 5 or No. 6 may be taken as the greatest possible strength. Various measures have been adopted by different authorities; for our purposes in this book it is proposed to classify them thus :

Strength 1. From softest possible to that required for one length of the table.

Strength 2. From one length to two lengths of the table.

Strength 3. From two lengths to three lengths of the table.

Strength 4. From three lengths to four lengths of the table, beyond which it is probably unnecessary to go. These

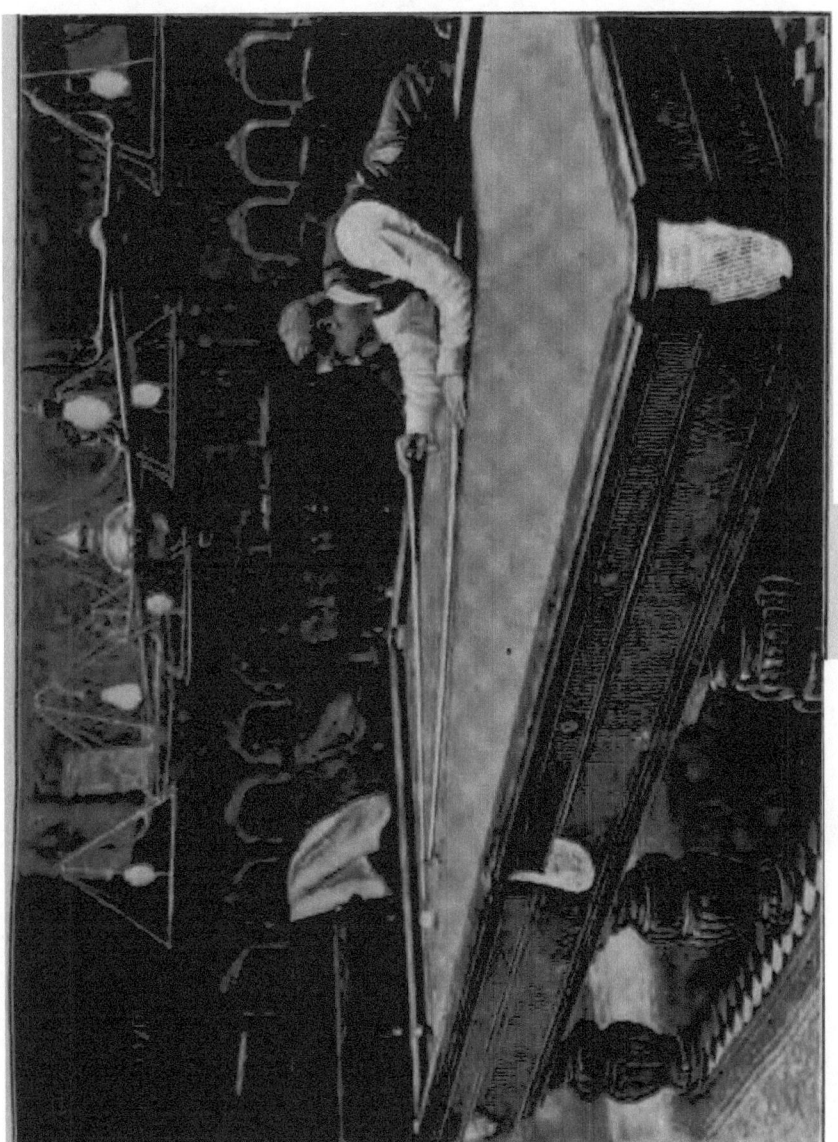

Using the Rest

ELEMENTARY: ONE-BALL PRACTICE

definitions may be further subdivided as desired : thus a very gentle stroke would be called a very slow or soft No. 1 ; a less slow one, medium No. 1 ; a stroke which required the strength to take a ball the length of the table, a full or free No. 1, which it is obvious reaches No. 2 strength ; where No. 1 ends No. 2 begins, and so on.

It is clear that the practice prescribed will familiarise the beginner with the various strengths, a matter which he will find greatly to his advantage.

When the ball cannot be comfortably reached by hand an artificial bridge, known as the rest, is employed. A short man requires it frequently, a tall man less often, but both should practise with it assiduously. A competent person will show a beginner the proper way of using it in a very short time. The handle of the rest should be nearly in the same line as the cue, only so far out of it as to permit of free delivery; the cue should be lightly held between forefinger and thumb, knuckles up, the elbow being raised level with the butt. The hand which holds the rest should lie on the table.

These are general rules, but they must on occasion be modified. The practice already defined will serve for strokes with the rest if the ball be placed sufficiently far from the cushion. The half-butt and long-butt should also be used. Before leaving this subject it is well to say that to be obliged to use the rest, and, worse still, the half-butt and long-butt, is at any time a drawback. This can be reduced to a minimum by learning to play with either hand ; a most useful accomplishment, by no means very difficult of attainment.

The following memorandum by Mr. Dudley D. Pontifex, who besides being a billiard-player of very high class is an expert at many other games, on the great importance of cultivating an almost mechanical accuracy in delivering the cue, and on the methods which he has followed in order to attain this end, will be read by proficients as well as beginners with both interest and profit. In essentials it agrees with the recommendations already given, and where it may seem to differ the variations are so small as not to require examination and explanation. Some interesting remarks on the styles of leading professional players will be found, and attention is justly directed to Roberts's admirable delivery of the cue, which is said to appear to be harder or stronger than it really is ; but one of the excellences of that great master's strokes is that they are habitually struck harder than is usual with other professionals ; the necessary compensations are, however, applied, and though the ball starts with considerably greater initial velocity than is usual, yet it does not necessarily travel farther or effect more. A heavy drag stroke played the length of the table by Roberts will travel nearly twice as fast as one struck by any other man, yet the object ball will often be found not to be harder hit.

The feat of screwing back to baulk from the red ball on the billiard spot, direct and without trick, is so remarkable that readers cannot fail to be much interested in a well-authenticated instance of the stroke. Besides Mr. Pontifex, William Seymour, (marker in 1895 at the Queen's Club) was present at the time, and has seen the gentleman do the stroke on many other occasions.

MEMORANDUM

By Dudley D. Pontifex

There is one characteristic which distinguishes games such as billiards and golf, and sharply divides them from others like cricket and tennis. While in the latter the stroke has to be made on a moving ball, in the former the ball is stationary. Instructions as to the method of making a stroke consequently vary in value in the two classes of games. The tiro at cricket or tennis is told to play a particular ball in a particular way, but is met with difficulties when he attempts to carry out the advice. The cricketer knows that he ought to play back or forward according to the length of the ball, but alas! too frequently is unable to decide until too late what the length of some particular ball is. At tennis it is much the same. The player knows well enough how the stroke should be made, but at the critical moment finds himself in such a position that it is utterly impossible to make a correct stroke. In these games the value of instructions is proportionable to the capacity of the player to adapt himself to the exigencies of the moment. It is quite different as regards billiards. Having once made up his mind as to the method to be adopted, there is absolutely nothing to prevent the player from carrying it into practical effect. He is not hurried for time. He is not called upon to make a sudden and, as it were, intuitive decision instantaneously. On the contrary, the table and balls are before him, and his opponent has to wait quietly until the turn is completed. Consequently the value of instructions, if there be any value in instructions, is relatively greatly enhanced in this class of game.

When one of our best professionals is playing, it is no uncommon thing to hear the remark made, 'What beautiful strength!' To my mind the excellence of a fine player's game lies not so much in his strength as in his accuracy. Given accuracy, strength will follow; at all events there is no reason why it should not. But strength without accuracy is useless, and even worse than useless. If a good player and a bad one meet, the latter usually has the better of the leaves. The reason is not difficult to discover, for the good player fails far more frequently from want of accuracy than from bad strength, and the balls are left fairly placed for his opponent. The bad player has little accuracy and less strength. He goes for his stroke, and chances position. After a score he leaves himself little, but if he fail he leaves little for his opponent. His play is characterised by a series of disjointed efforts.

But, although the good player fails more often from want of accuracy than from bad strength, he does not, unless the balls are very close together, try for exact strength. To use a well-understood phrase, he tries to get them there or thereabouts. Take a very fine player, and let him play from baulk with the other two balls nicely placed in the middle of the table, and let him play two breaks with the balls so placed. It is almost certain that after the third stroke, probably the second, the breaks will branch out differently. The good player only tries to place the balls about where he means. If he be at all successful, he will have the choice of playing one of perhaps half a dozen different strokes. Not one of these half-dozen strokes is, it may be, difficult; and then he has to consider which will leave him the best break, and if there be three or more leaving an equally good game he takes the easiest. What is deserving of observation is that, whichever he selects, he usually makes the stroke and approximately carries out his idea.

.It is this deadly accuracy which is so noticeable in the play of the best professionals. How have they obtained it? First and chiefly by years of constant and assiduous practice, secondly by a correct mechanical style. Nothing can take the place of the former. No amount of teaching will be the equivalent of strong individual effort extended over a length of time. The player who really excels at billiards must have given a large amount of time to it. He who plays a wonderful game, and yet hardly ever touches a cue, exists only in the imagination of the incompetent novelist. But, although nothing can compensate for hard practice, something may be done for the beginner by teaching him how to obtain a correct style. To avoid errors is the surest and quickest way to real progress, and to thoroughly grasp the idea of a true mechanical style is the most important lesson in billiards. There is no one style that can be said to be the only correct and proper one. If the best half-dozen players be watched, it will be seen that they all differ in various ways from one another. The position of their heads, and the way in which they hold the cue, are often entirely different. One thing, however, may be noted, that however much they differ from one another, they are true to themselves. Each man keeps rigidly to his own style. His position and his manner of delivering the stroke are constant so far as circumstances permit, and this is the lesson which the amateur may properly take to heart. Billiards is more of a mechanical game than anything else, and, because the mechanical part of it is so important, nothing can take the place of continual practice on right lines. And even that which may have been a defective style originally may, by becoming habitual, lose half its injuriousness. The beginner, however, wants to avoid defects so that he may have nothing subsequently to unlearn, and he wants to know the nearest road to the best game of which he is capable. When he has once got a clear idea of what a correct style is, he is next door to getting the thing itself. And it is worth some little trouble to get. For not only will his general progress at the game be more rapid, but he will find the utility of it at a critical moment. Some pernicious trick or mannerism may not be particularly injurious on ordinary occasions, but when the stress of a match comes it is apt to be fatal. It is then that the man with an easy and correct style finds half his work done for him, as it were.

It is by no means an uncommon thing to see what may be called the pump-handle style, where the cue, instead of moving horizontally or nearly so, is at the commencement of the stroke lifted high at the butt, and then brought forward with a circular sweep. This makes it a matter of no little skill in itself to hit the ball at all correctly, and yet we see players who apparently are not satisfied with the ordinary difficulties of billiards, but must add a quite superfluous one to every stroke.

Most of these eccentric players must be to some extent aware of their eccentricities, and a very little reflection would show that they are quite unnecessary and may be harmful.

Apart from any theoretical consideration of the matter, a casual observation of really good players proves that they do not indulge in these atrocities. In fact, our best players are, almost without exception, easy, graceful players, and distinctly the best break I ever saw North play was at the same time the quickest and least demonstrative of any I have seen made by that player. The play of John Roberts is almost above criticism, and his style is at once the delight and despair of all. Diggle, Dawson, and Richards, more especially the last, are charming players to watch. They who can remember Cook at his best will recall with delight a style that was in the opinion of many unrivalled. An imperturbable temper that nothing appeared to ruffle, a nerve that never seemed to fail, a touch always firm and crisp, yet often using a strength so delicate that he seemed to require instruments more accurate than the best manufacturers could supply—these were some of the features of a game that ever had a great fascination for the spectator.

A few words may not be out of place on the benefit of private practice, *i.e.* practice by oneself. I believe from a tolerably wide experience that they are exceptional, very exceptional, who can keep on improving without having had, at some time or other, a good deal of private practice. How many men there are who play their two or three hours every day, and yet at the end of fifteen years are little, if any, better! It is because their energies are being entirely absorbed by the immediate contest. If they have a fault in style, they have no time to correct it. They cannot make up their minds to court present defeat for a future gain. They play the same old game with the same bad result year in and year out. The least innovation on their stereotyped game will probably result in failure, and perhaps defeat, and is therefore rejected. After a time they come to accept their game as the best of which they are capable, and when they see really good play they admire it, but never appear to dream of taking a hint from it for their own improvement.

A short time given to private practice would do much for such a one. Here there is no opponent to distract, no dread of consequences. The greatest novelty, even to the playing of a losing hazard at dead slow strength the length of the table, may be attempted fearlessly. But this is not all. Not only may every kind of stroke be attempted without any attaching penalty, but if there be a fault of which the player is conscious he may now correct it. His attention is now concentrated upon the one point, and it is wonderful how soon that which has become habitual may be changed by steady determined suppression. Billiards again, at least to play one's best game, is very much a question of confidence, and confidence is born of familiarity. He who has played a particular stroke in a particular way a hundred times successfully in private practice, not only feels that he can do that stroke in that way in a match, but that it is his best chance of doing the stroke at all. He is in a way compelled into the better class of game.

Probably no amateur is in the least likely to go through the years of continuous labour that the best professionals have given to the game. But in many instances he may, by giving some consideration to the matter and taking a little trouble, acquire a greater degree of accuracy than has hitherto been associated with his game. Accuracy in play means accuracy in striking, and the player has to aim at hitting ball after ball with the precision of a machine. Of course one seldom or never gets two strokes running exactly alike, but the various movements of the body which precede and accompany the delivery of the stroke may be and should be alike. This uniformity of style is the groundwork of accuracy, and it is by a recognition of the various movements and a careful observance of them that the player may obtain a correct mechanical style. He should once for all definitely decide what is the best style for him to adopt, and, having decided, should strictly observe it with unfailing regularity. It is absolutely fatal to keep chopping and changing in the endeavour to copy a better player. In all probability that which is copied has nothing to do with the excellence of the play. It is perhaps some little trick which is peculiar to the man, the result of his build or of his early billiard education. Most of us have known some friend who, after seeing John Roberts give one of his wonderful exhibitions of skill, has attempted to imitate his rapidity of play. The last state of that person is worse than his first. We cannot all play our best in the same way. Some men are naturally quick players, others lose whatever merit they may have in the attempt to hurry through their stroke. Usually, the better practice a man is in the quicker he plays, but, whether he play fast or slow, he should always play naturally and at the same pace. If he be playing badly, conscious hurrying over or dwelling on the stroke will not mend matters. The reason for the bad play must be sought elsewhere. Usually the internal machinery has in some way gone wrong. But the last thing a man cares to admit is any failing in himself. It is far more pleasant to attribute his ill success to something else. Still, if his style be not radically wrong, and if during one of these seasons of depression he attempts to vary it, his game will surely suffer when the causes which led to his temporary deterioration have passed away.

If I venture to give some advice, it is with a double motive ; first, to illustrate my meaning how, by a careful attention to details, uniformity of style may be obtained, and, second, in the hope that it may in some respects be found useful by beginners. But before doing so I should like to say a few words as to what I conceive to be the real utility of advice. What is too often the case is this. The beginner tries to recollect before every stroke all he has learnt, and laboriously endeavours to reduce each and every rule into practice at the same time. Some of these rules may be the exact opposite of his previous method. The consequence is that this attempt at wholesale assimilation causes the player to look like a trussed-up fowl, uncomfortable to himself and unnatural to others. He should remember that that which is ungainly in style is usually wrong, always superfluous.

Rules may be good enough in themselves, but if there be a grave difference between them and our former method there will always be a difficulty about their immediate application. There is no authority for the opinion that the world was made in a day, and even at games time must be allowed to bring about the desired result. Too great insistence upon the observance of several rules at the same time distresses and discourages the player. But if he will get, more especially in the intervals of play, a clear mental recognition of the rules which he believes to be specially applicable to himself, he will find that they will presently begin to work out in practice. This is not only a more pleasant but a better way. Without any conscious effort, the player finds that the mind is beginning to direct and control the bodily movements. The result thus arrives in an apparently natural way, and when it so comes it comes to stay. That this is the best use to which advice can be put is an opinion derived from an experience more or less intimate with a variety of games.

No exact formula can be laid down with regard to position. This is precisely one of those cases in which some latitude must be allowed for a man's make and shape. Two points, however, should be borne in mind. To state them in their natural order they are, first, that the player should always, so far as circumstances permit, assume the same relative position as between himself, his own ball, and the line of direction. A useful general rule is the following. When the player takes his position opposite his own ball with his left leg advanced as is the usual manner, the line of direction if prolonged backwards through the centre of his ball would pass through the centre of his body. As he settles to his stroke, the body naturally sways a little to the left, leaving the right arm free to swing in the proper direction. Secondly, the position should be a firm one. The advantage of this will be more particularly felt in any game in which nerves play a part. If there be any tendency to unsteadiness in the player's position, it will then be emphasised. The body should be kept as motionless as possible, the feet being firmly placed and the right leg straight.

It is not easy to recognise the true natural angle [1] under all

---

[1] Often called the half-ball angle, both definitions being very inaccurate; but they are in common use, and generally understood.

its different phases, and the frequent failure of even the best players at long losing hazards shows this. Constant practice is the only teacher, and the plan of having for private play two strips of wood joined together at the proper angle—and which was, I believe, first introduced by Joseph Bennett—is very useful. The angle is more sharply defined, and therefore easier of recognition, if taken through some fixed point, and this point should be the centre of the player's ball. The angle should be taken to the centre of the pocket.

It is almost a rarity to find a really good baulk-line player, and in some cases it is quite the weakest point in a man's game. That this should be so seems strange, seeing that the player has such a wide range within which to place his own ball. It is, I think, often this very option of choice of position that causes the stroke to be missed. The player places his ball, perhaps, quite correctly for the first long loser he has, but misses it through hitting his own ball falsely. He does not attribute his failure to its proper cause, but thinks he has placed his own ball wrongly. Next time he puts it a little wider or narrower as the case may be, and if he happen to put on by accident the proper amount of side and does the stroke, he is almost worse off than ever, for the first time he does hit his own ball truly he comes to grief. By this time he has got an entirely wrong estimate of what the true natural angle is, and it may be a matter of several days before he can do the stroke with any certainty. Another point may be remarked. If the player use only his left eye in play, he should judge the angle only with his left eye; if he use both eyes, then judge with both eyes; but if he uses the right eye to take the angle and the left eye to play, when he settles to his stroke the angle will often appear wrong, and he will become confused as to what the correct natural angle really is. This probably arises from the fact that with most people the focus of the two eyes is not identical.

Whether the cue should be held only by the fingers, or in the hollow of the hand, may be matter of opinion, but there is no doubt it should be held lightly, not gripped. Any rigidity of the muscles tends to impair the easy pendulum swing so essential to accurate play. Some people seem to think it necessary to grip the cue when making a screw. The point is easily susceptible of practical demonstration if they will only condescend to hit the ball in the proper place.

With many players, again, the position of the left hand appears to be a matter of supreme indifference. They place it on the table anyhow, and almost without taking a glance at the stroke. Now it is all very well to say 'Look at John Roberts. He doesn't worry about these things,' but we are not, most of us at least, of the calibre of John Roberts. His easy and graceful style is deceptive. If anyone will take the trouble to contrast the face of the man with his manner of play, it will be apparent how thoroughly concentrated is his mind on the game. He is the consummate artist who conceals the difficulty of the stroke under the ease of its execution. For most players, and all beginners, it is advisable to pay some little attention to the position of the left hand. Obviously it is of importance. If it has to be moved, however slightly, after the player has settled to his stroke, the result will be a loss of accuracy. It should be advanced with care, by which I do not mean with wearisome laboriousness, to the player's ball, the eye being steadily kept on the line of direction, or, better still, on the exact spot on the object ball it is desired to hit.

The cue from tip to butt should be in one straight line with the line of direction. It may be thought that this is always the case, but a close observation will show that very frequently the cue along its length is by no means in a straight line with the point aimed at. I have found it most useful to bear this rule in mind, especially when beginning practice after a long absence from the billiard-table.

The player should not hurry up from the table after delivering his stroke. The fault indicated may easily become a habit, and a very bad one. It may be often observed among the more impatient class of players. It may cause the body to move at the very moment when it is most essential it should be quite steady, viz. at the moment of the cue's contact with the ball.

A few more hints may be useful to some. Much of billiards is played before settling to the stroke. This may at first sight appear an absurd statement, but it contains an important truth. If the player have a clearly defined idea not only of what stroke he is going for, but how it is to be made, much of the difficulty is already overcome; but if he go down to his stroke, and then have an elaborate consultation with himself as to what is to be done, the process is not only harassing to his opponent but detrimental to himself. Once having decided on the stroke, he should go for it unhesitatingly, and as though no other stroke were possible. To play one game, at the same time having a lingering partiality for another, is not usually attended with success.

The height of the player and the length of his arms will to a considerable extent determine where he should hold the cue so that he may combine sufficient power with the greatest attainable accuracy. It must not, therefore, be held too far back. This may cause a slight loss of power, but that is of very small importance. The bad play so often seen in amateur billiards is not usually to be attributed to any want of power of execution.

I have never known a professional do a stroke which most amateurs could not copy, though I have known one instance of an amateur being able to do that which probably no professional living could do. The feat deserves to be recorded. The gentleman was an undergraduate at Cambridge, and it was said that he could from baulk screw back off the red on the spot into baulk again. One day I asked him to do it for my edification, and at the third attempt he succeeded. The balls used were two of the usual set with which we ordinarily played. He used his own cue, which was one of the usual pattern of English cues. The white came straight back without touching a cushion. There are many persons besides myself who have seen him do it, but I have never heard an authenticated case of any other person who could perform the feat.

On the face of it, it seems wrong that a man of six feet and one of five feet six inches should hold cues of the same length in the same place, and a slight consideration of the nature of a proper stroke will show very good reasons for not holding the cue too long. The stroke itself should be made by, as nearly as may be, a horizontal motion of the cue. Any depression of the cue tip has a tendency to make the ball take a slight curve. There are strokes when it is desirable to sharply raise the butt for the very purpose of making one's own ball describe a curve before contact with the object ball, and such strokes are sometimes very useful when the pocket is a narrow one. But as a general rule the movement of the cue should be as nearly horizontal as circumstances allow. Now, if the cue be held too long for thorough control over it, as the player's hand goes back before delivering the stroke it will take an upward direction, and one of two things must take place when the stroke is made. If, during the forward movement, the cue work in a plane, it will be depressed at the moment of contact with the ball; but if at the moment of contact it be horizontal, or nearly so, it will have described a slightly circular movement. This is one of the things to be avoided, for the cue should work like a piston-rod.

The bridge should be a short bridge rather than a long one. What is meant by a short bridge is a short distance between the bridge itself and the player's ball. Too long a bridge must necessarily diminish accuracy of hitting. The stroke itself should come from the arm alone, and as much as possible from the elbow, the movement of the shoulder being kept within the narrowest limits. However delicate, it should be a clean, crisp blow, avoiding the least suspicion of a push. In this respect it is exceedingly instructive to watch John Roberts play. He appears to strike the ball so hard, even in his close game, that one is at a loss to understand how it stops so quickly—the fact being that the ball is struck so firmly, and so clean, as to give the appearance of a harder stroke than in reality it is. It is a very unusual thing to see an amateur strike his ball crisply when using delicate strengths. Not only should the angle be judged, but aim should be taken through the centre of the player's ball. This applies to every stroke not less than a half ball. For all ordinary strokes—excepting, of course, screws, &c.—the ball should be struck, whether with side or without, exactly half-way up. The ball when so struck runs truer.

One last word of advice. It is—simplify your game. If you can take your choice of two games, one which looks promising but with possible complications, the other simple and obvious, choose the latter. Some two or three years ago Dawson was for this reason a most instructive player for the amateur. His game was so simple that he never appeared to be in a difficulty. He has somewhat changed its character since, but I question if he has ever played better than he did then. In this respect John Roberts is the last player the amateur should attempt to copy. His game is full of complications, but he gets rid of them with an ease and a celerity that fairly astonish the onlookers. He is out of a difficulty almost before one has recognised that there is one. Sometimes he seems to fairly revel in them, and deliberately to make them for the pleasure of getting out of them. It is certainly wonderfully attractive, but the percentage of men who could play such a game with success would be infinitesimal.

If this memorandum appear too didactic, I can only apologise to my readers. It must necessarily assume that character to some extent. But, in truth, the advice is not meant for good players. It may be that there are some fine players who have never consciously observed any rules, but have naturally adopted a correct style. They are facile players, but they know not the pleasure which comes from attacking and overcoming difficulties. There are others, quite as fond of the game, who find the road to even partial success a somewhat stony one. These hints, or some of them, may perhaps be of use to such. One thing is certain. Not even the most perfect rules or the most undeniable instructions can of themselves make a good player. They cannot take the place of hard work. All they can do is to help the beginner over some of the difficulties others have met with, and so save him time.

The Bridge (*bouclé*)

MOTION, IMPACT, AND DIVISION OF BALLS:
TWO-BALL PRACTICE

THE practice prescribed in the preceding chapter had for its chief object the attainment of certainty in striking ball 1 truly in the centre; we now proceed to study some of the elementary facts concerning the impact of one ball with another.

In the first place, the conditions of impact should be recognised, and what is termed the division of balls must be explained.

Now, for practical purposes the cloth and bed of the table are level, and the balls are of the same size; hence when they touch one another the point of contact is invariably on the line of their greatest horizontal circumference, which, as all know, is precisely at half their height. It will hereafter be shown that ball 1 may be caused to leap, and so strike ball 2 above this; but for present purposes, when a plain stroke alone is being considered, it may be accepted as a fact that the point of impact is always at half the ball's height. That fixes the location of impact vertically; but horizontally it is evident that there is considerable latitude. Ball 1 may hit ball 2 either precisely full, when the centre of one is played on the centre of the other, or it may strike either to the right or left of the centre of ball 2; the limit on either side being the finest possible touch. The accompanying figure will show what is meant. When ball 1 hits ball 2 full, at the moment of impact it occupies the position 1″; and the part of 2 which can be struck by a ball situated at 1 is from P″ to P; if ball 1

OPENING THE GAME.

TWO-BALL PRACTICE

occupies the position 1', then the part of 2 which may be touched is restricted to that marked P" P'; but should ball 1 be placed at 1", then the only point on 2 it can touch is P". Therefore the nearer 1 is to 2 the less of the latter can be struck, and the further away the more.

As regards the division of balls, for the English game at any rate, the simpler it is the better. The larger balls on a smaller table, as used in the French game, admit of more minute. subdivision than do our smaller balls, which may be, and often are, further from the player's eye. To attempt a division which the eye cannot easily appreciate is a mistake. For purposes of play both balls 1 and 2 must be divided; and although at this early stage of the manual we are not concerned with the division of ball 1 (for all practice at present is confined to centre strokes), yet it is convenient now to record the divisions of both balls.

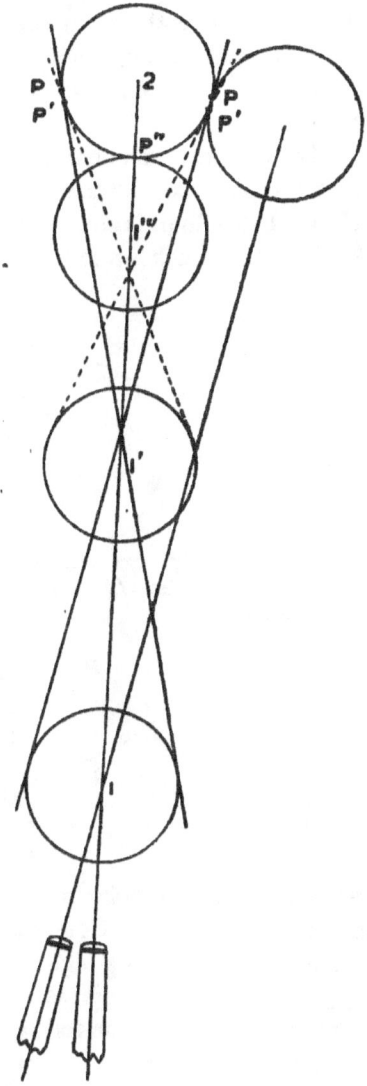

Fig. 1

Ball 1 is divided by its vertical and horizontal diameters

into four parts. The centre stroke is delivered at C, and is of all strokes by far the commonest and most important.

A ball struck high and right is struck in the sector C A E ; low and left in C D B ; high and left in C A D ; low and right in C E B.

The vertical and horizontal lines are divided from the centre where they intersect, into four equal parts each way. Thus a ball ¼ high is struck on the line C A at the point marked ¼ ; ½ low is struck on C B at the point marked ½ ; ¾ right is

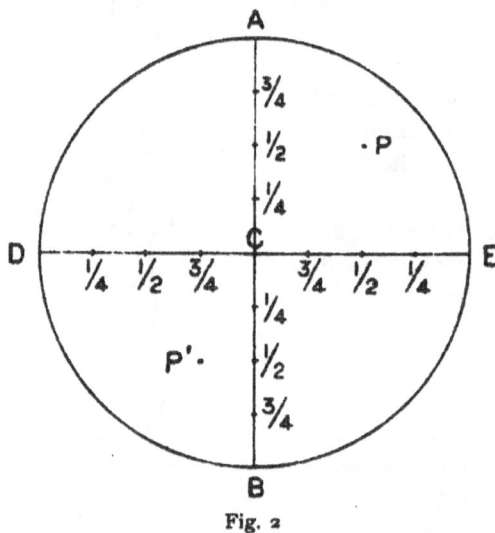

Fig. 2

struck on CE at the point marked ¾ ; ¼ left is struck on C D at the point marked ¼. Combinations of these divisions are of course possible: thus ½ high and right would indicate a point P ; ¾ left and ½ low is represented by P'. That division is quite as minute as the eye can follow ; indeed, for general purposes it will probably suffice to indicate the sector only ; to say, for example, ball 1 should be struck high and right.

In respect to ball 2 the matter is different ; it cannot, as has already been shown, be struck save on the line C C'A, the height

TWO-BALL PRACTICE

of its centre c′ above the table, therefore that line alone requires division. c′ is the centre, and division is made therefrom in equal portions of one-fourth of the radius. In the accompanying figure ball 1, whose centre is c, is shown in the position it occupies at the moment of impact, when a half-ball stroke has been played; the centre of ball 1 is aimed at the edge of ball 2, and the point of impact is at ½, between c and c′. No stroke is more important to master, or indeed easier, than the half-ball, because the point of aim is sharply

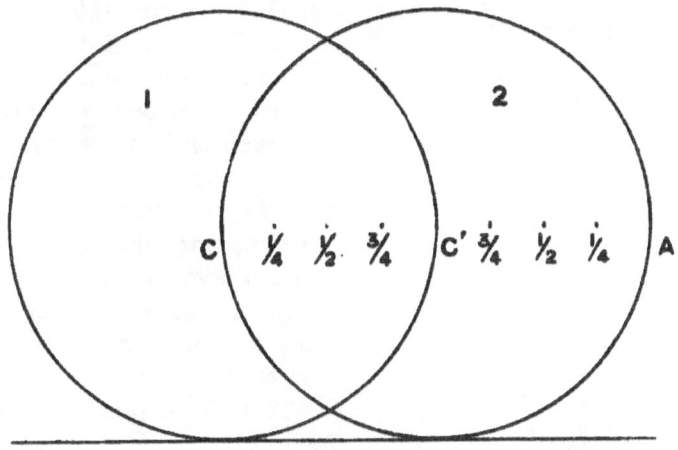

SURFACE OF TABLE

Fig. 3

defined; the line of the cue's axis passing through the centre of ball 1 and touching the edge of ball 2, and this edge being distinct affords a better target than an imaginary point on the ball's surface. The next easiest stroke as regards aim is when centre is played on centre, or ball 1 full on ball 2 ; ¾ and ¼ being both more difficult of aim ; but resolute practice will soon diminish the trouble. Here an important matter should be noticed, which is the divergence between the point of aim and that of impact. The two coincide in one case only—*i.e.*

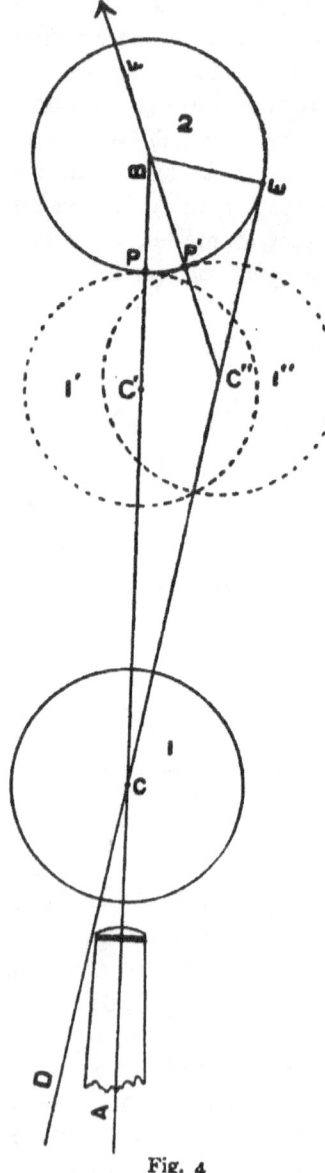

Fig. 4

when ball 1 is played full on ball 2; in every other instance the point of ball 2 aimed at is not struck. This fact is often overlooked and leads to many failures. A player sees the precise point on 2 which he desires to strike in order to pocket it; he aims accurately at that point, delivers his stroke, but fails to score. He is probably puzzled to account for the failure, but ultimately attributes it to personal error. Yet it very often is not so as far as the delivery of cue is concerned; the error may lie in not recognising that he had to aim at a point other than that which he desired to hit in order that impact should be correct.

This will be plainly evident from fig. 4.

When ball 1 is played full on 2 the line of the cue's axis A B passes through the centres of both balls, and the points of aim and of impact are both at P.

Next suppose it played half-ball; then D E is the line of the cue's axis and E the point of aim; but, so far from E being touched, if we suppose ball 1 arrested in its course at the

TWO-BALL PRACTICE

moment of reaching 2, then its position will be that of the dotted circle 1″, whose centre is c″, and p′ is the point of impact. For any stroke between full and half-ball the point of impact will lie between p and p′; between half-ball and the extreme of fineness the point of impact will lie beyond p′ in the direction of e.

Ball 2 being struck by ball 1 at p′ must travel in the direction p′ b f, the line from the point of impact passing through b the centre. There is practically no departure from this rule. Hence it follows that if it be desired that ball 2 should travel in the direction b f, say to a pocket, imagine a line from the pocket passing through the ball's centre; this cuts the circumference at p′, which is manifestly the point which must be struck by ball 1. Where is the centre of ball 1 to be aimed at in order that p′ may be struck? Produce the imaginary line f b p′ to c″, making p′ c″ equal to b p′, or in other words equal to the radius of the ball. If the centre of ball 1, c, be aimed on c″, ball 2 must be struck at p′ and must travel in the direction required.

Pray realise that it is impossible to hit ball 2 at the point aimed at save when the stroke is full; in every other case the aim must be beyond the point of impact, and the rule above given will enable anyone to determine precisely where aim should be taken.

When a ball is struck by the cue its first impulse is to slide forward, and if there were no friction between the ball and the cloth it would do so till arrested by other causes; but as there always is this friction, the lower part of the ball is thereby retarded, and the result is the rolling or revolving motion with which all are familiar. This will be further considered when the subject of rotation is discussed, but it is mentioned here as the cause of certain effects which will be observed in some of the strokes recommended for practice. When one ball impinges on another the immediate result is a greater or lesser flattening of both surfaces at the point of impact; this is instantaneously followed by recoil,[1] the result of each ball reassuming its spherical

[1] Or *restitution*, the effect of *compression*.

form. The greater the strength of stroke the greater the flattening and the greater the recoil; the converse likewise holds good.

Further, the force or strength with which ball 1 strikes ball 2 is immediately divided on impact; if ball 2 be struck full it appears to acquire from ball 1 the whole of its energy save that due to naturally developed rotation, the result being that ball 2 travels fast whilst ball 1 remains comparatively stationary. If the distance between the two balls be very small, little rotation is acquired and ball 1 transmits its motion to ball 2 and stops on or near the spot which that ball occupied; if the distance be considerable, ball 1 acquires rotation which, overcoming the recoil on impact, causes it to travel slowly in its original direction. When impact is other than full, ball 1 parts with more or less of its force, which is transmitted to ball 2. What the one loses the other gains.

These general remarks will seem to many self-evident and superfluous; to others they may prove difficult to realise and distasteful; but students, whether beginners or those who have already acquaintance with the game, may rest assured that a careful consideration of them can do no harm and may be of much advantage; for practice is assisted by an intelligent appreciation of the behaviour of balls under certain conditions; in short, by a consideration of cause and effect.

For practice: place ball 1 on the centre of the **D** on the baulk-line, put ball 2 a foot up the table in the central line, play 1 full on 2 with varying strength, at first with strength to carry 2 to the top cushion; the truth of the stroke will be shown by 2 passing over all the spots in the central line and 1 following slowly in the same line for a short distance. When tolerable certainty is acquired play the same stroke harder, and if correctly struck ball 2 will return from the top cushion and meet ball 1, kiss as it is called, in the central line. The stroke can be made more difficult by placing ball 2 further up the table, say on the centre spot, and playing as before, and again by placing it on the pyramid spot. This practice, though it may

TWO-BALL PRACTICE

seem uninteresting, is most useful; it combines and continues that recommended for one ball with that required for truth of stroke on another. It also, as will hereafter be shown, is directly useful in the matter of cannons, hence it should be assiduously practised.

Next set ball 2 upon the central line at such a distance from the baulk-line as the player can imagine its division described on page 133, and play ball 1 so as to make three-quarter, half, and quarter-ball strokes with some confidence. This distance will no doubt vary with the stature and sight of the player, but 2 feet may be tried as about average. If P, P', P'' be the points of impact for the various divisions, ball 2 will, after the strokes, travel in the directions R, R', R'', each being the prolongation of a line from the point of impact through the centre. Ball 1 will behave differently according to the strength with which it is struck; what is always true is that it will travel in a contrary direction to

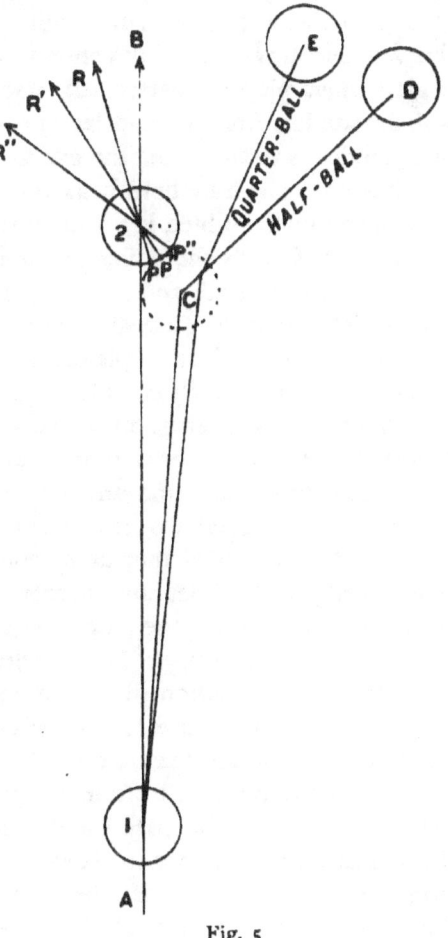

Fig. 5

ball 2. If the one ball goes to the left after impact the other will go to the right. Played with strength 1 or 2, impact being at P, ball 1 will follow through the space which ball 2 covered, and will stop slightly to the right of the line A B. With impact at P' or a half-ball stroke, ball 1 will deviate further from the line A B, and travel in the direction D, A C D being the half-ball angle; when played quarter-ball, impact being at P", ball 1 will deviate less from A B and travel towards E. The object of this practice is to accustom the eye to recognise approximately the directions taken by both balls after impact.

A small matter which is a little obscure connected with the language of billiards should here be noticed. In placing ball 1 for a stroke, it is usual, and generally desirable, to select a spot from which the angle 1 C D shall be what is known as the half-ball angle, and certainty in play is greatly based on the power of recognising this position. Consequently in time players, perhaps unconsciously, refer almost every stroke to that angle as a standard. If a hazard or cannon is on the table, they consider for a moment whether the angle contained between the two paths of ball 1 is greater or less than the half-ball angle, and to the best of their ability they apply compensations to meet the difference, playing fuller and harder when the angle is less, finer and slower when the angle is greater, until a following stroke becomes necessary. Nevertheless, the universal custom is to define the situation when the angle is smaller as *wider*, and when the angle is greater as *narrower*. Thus the position 1 C D is called wider than 1 C E. Clearly it is so only as regards the deviation of ball 1 from the prolongation of its original path—that is, from the path which would have been followed if there had been no impact—consequently the angle of deviation must be defined as that between the new actual path of ball 1 and the path that would have been described if the deviation had not taken place. This being accepted, the ordinary use of the terms *wider* and *narrower* is appropriate.

In this and in all diagrams as far as possible the lines followed by the centres of balls are shown ; hence, as the centres cannot touch each other or the cushions, the lines do not reach to the surface of either, but are necessarily short of the point of impact by the length of the ball's radius. Ball 1, after impact other than full, describes a curve due to the forces to which it is subject ; this is greater in proportion to the strength of stroke, and though in practice its effect must not be neglected, it is not ordinarily shown in the diagrams, which do not pretend to abso-

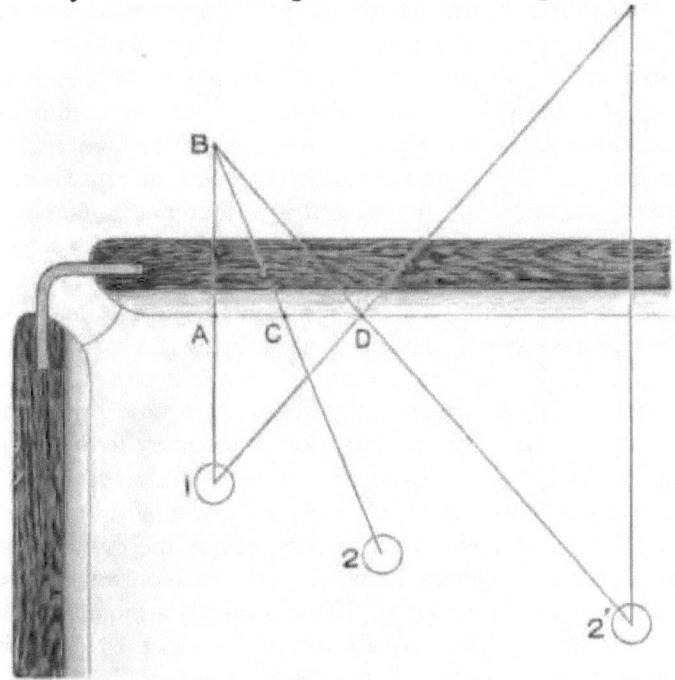

Fig. 6

lute accuracy, but merely to such measure of correctness as is required for practical purposes. An illustration of the curve, and a warning when its existence must not be overlooked, will be found in Chapter V.

From the strokes recommended in Chapter III. for practice it will have been learnt that in a general way a ball played against a cushion will return therefrom, so that the angle of reflexion shall be nearly equal to the angle of incidence. A useful two-ball practice based on this is to place balls 1 and 2 on the table and endeavour to play on 2, having first struck a cushion.

The difficulty is to determine the point on the cushion on which 1 must impinge so as to rebound on 2.

The solution is approximately :—From ball 1 let fall 1 A perpendicular to the cushion A C D ; produce 1 A to B, making A B = 1 A. Join B with the centre of 2 ; where that line cuts the cushion at C is the point required. Play 1 so that it shall strike C and it will rebound on 2. Similarly, if the second ball occupy the position 2' the line from B to its centre intersects the cushion at D ; ball 1 played to touch the cushion at D will travel to 2'. In a game of course the cushion must not be marked, but in practice it will at first be found advantageous to mark the spot sufficiently to guide the stroke and educate the eye. This is easily done by placing a piece of chalk on the wooden frame of the cushion just behind the spot to be hit, thus doing away with the need of marking the cushion with chalk, which it is well to avoid. When it is necessary to mark the cloth of bed or cushion, pipeclay such as tailors use is preferable to chalk. Special attention is necessary to two facts : first, the angle of reflexion varies with the strength ; that is, a soft stroke will come off very nearly at the same angle as that of incidence, whilst with a hard stroke there is a perceptible difference ; second, the point on the cushion which should be hit must not be aimed at. This is merely a modification of what has already been explained with reference to the points of aim and of impact. Fig. 7 shows how very far a ball on the line 1P played, *i.e.* aimed at P, is from hitting that point ; instead of doing so it strikes the cushion at T ; hence allowance must be made in aiming, the length allowed on the cushion diminishing as the angle approaches a right angle. When the stroke is at a right angle to the cushion the points P and T coincide and no allowance is required.

One reason why the angle of reflexion varies with the strength is that, on impact with the cushion, the ball, being harder than the rubber, indents it - -makes a sort of cup, in fact, deeper as the stroke is stronger. Friction with the cloth of the cushion has also some effect on the angle, and there may be other causes at work ; fortunately, it is probable that

TWO-BALL PRACTICE

one to some extent counteracts another. This practice from a cushion is interesting as well as useful; at first the beginner will be satisfied if he hits ball 2 anywhere and anyhow; but soon he will be able to hit it on one side or the other, as he may wish, when the distance ball 1 has to travel is not very

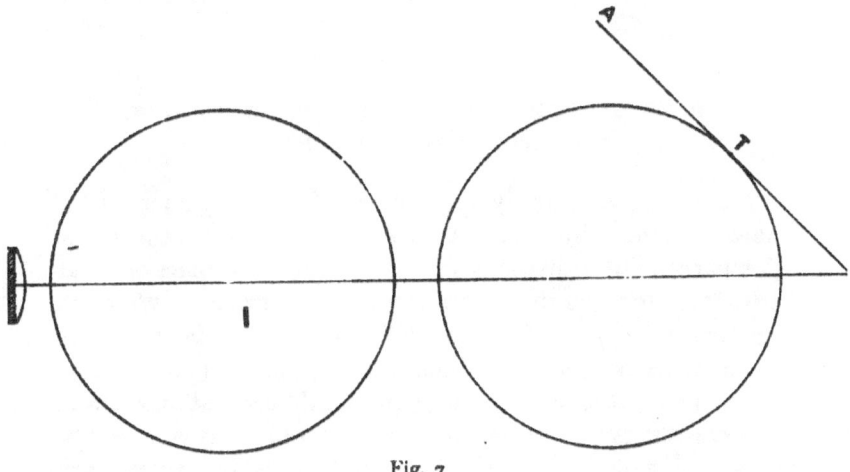

Fig. 7

great. Hereafter both cannons and hazards will be mentioned, which must be played *bricole*, or off a cushion before ball 2 is struck, and the practice proposed will make their execution fairly easy and certain. We conclude this chapter, which has covered important ground, with four illustrations of the division of ball 2 at the moment of impact. A shows ball 1 applied to 2 for a quarter-ball stroke, B for a half ball, C for a three-quarter-ball, and D for a full-ball stroke; the phases varying between partial and total eclipse.

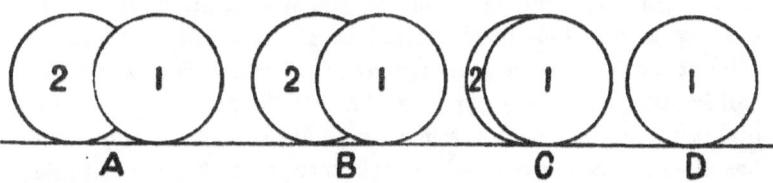

Fig. 8

PLAIN STROKES, WINNING AND LOSING HAZARDS,
CANNONS : THREE-BALL PRACTICE

By the practice already recommended, the beginner should have become fairly able to strike ball 1 in the centre, and familiar with the divisions of ball 2 ; he may therefore with advantage proceed to play natural or plain strokes. We prefer the term plain, partly because, ball 1 being struck in the centre, no rotation beyond that which is self-acquired or spontaneous is communicated by the cue, and partly because one stroke deserves the name natural as much as another. It is as natural for a ball struck on its side to rotate round its vertical axis as it is for a ball struck in the centre to have no such rotation.

In billiards plain strokes cover a vast field ; most of the certainties, or strokes which should seldom be missed, come under that definition. Their number is infinite, and it is impossible to give diagrams of more than a few typical examples. The student can, without great effort, multiply and vary them at will, and it is desirable that he should do so, altering the strength and noting the behaviour of each ball after the stroke. He will thus learn more than he can possibly acquire from any book, however excellent, and will profit much if his practice is occasionally supervised by a competent instructor.

Let us begin with winning hazards. Place ball 2 on the centre spot ; it is then opposite the middle pockets. Choose one of them into which the ball is to be played. From what has already been explained, it is known that the ball should

A Disputed Score.

travel on a line drawn from its centre to the centre of the pocket—that is, from C to A (fig. 1); also that the point of impact must be where that line prolonged meets the circumference at B, and that the centre of ball 1 must therefore, at the moment of striking, be at P, B P being equal to B C, or the radius of the balls. No matter where ball 1 may be situated, its centre has to be played on P in order that the winning hazard may be perfectly made.

Set ball 1 on the prolongation of A C, which is the line of the cue's axis. The player must place himself accordingly, and aim full at ball 2. The stroke is precisely similar to that recommended for practice over the spots, but easier, as the distances are shorter. It should be played with various strengths. With a soft No. 1, ball 2 will roll into the pocket, ball 1 following a few inches on the same path. If it diverge there is error in the stroke, and endeavour should be made to correct it. That is, the player should not be satisfied with the mere winning hazard, which is very simple, but should by watching the path of the balls, satisfy himself that the stroke was true. With No. 2 strength, or a free No. 2, ball 1 will follow on, and eventually drop into the same pocket.

When tolerable certainty has been acquired, ball 1 may be moved to $1'$, $1''$, &c., either to the right or left of the original position. No good can result from giving precise measurements for the various situations of ball 1; it does not, indeed, greatly matter where it is set, so long as the player can reach it with comfort; what is obligatory is that its centre must pass over the point P. The limit of the stroke is when the position 1^n is reached; thence, if correctly played, point B will just be touched, and no motion to ball 2 be communicated. Hence, when the path of ball 1 before impact is at right angles to that which 2 must travel, the winning hazard is impossible. In other words, a right-angled cut is impossible; such strokes sometimes seem to be made, but the explanation will, on examination, be found in the size and shape of the pockets. These winning hazards should be practised into both middle

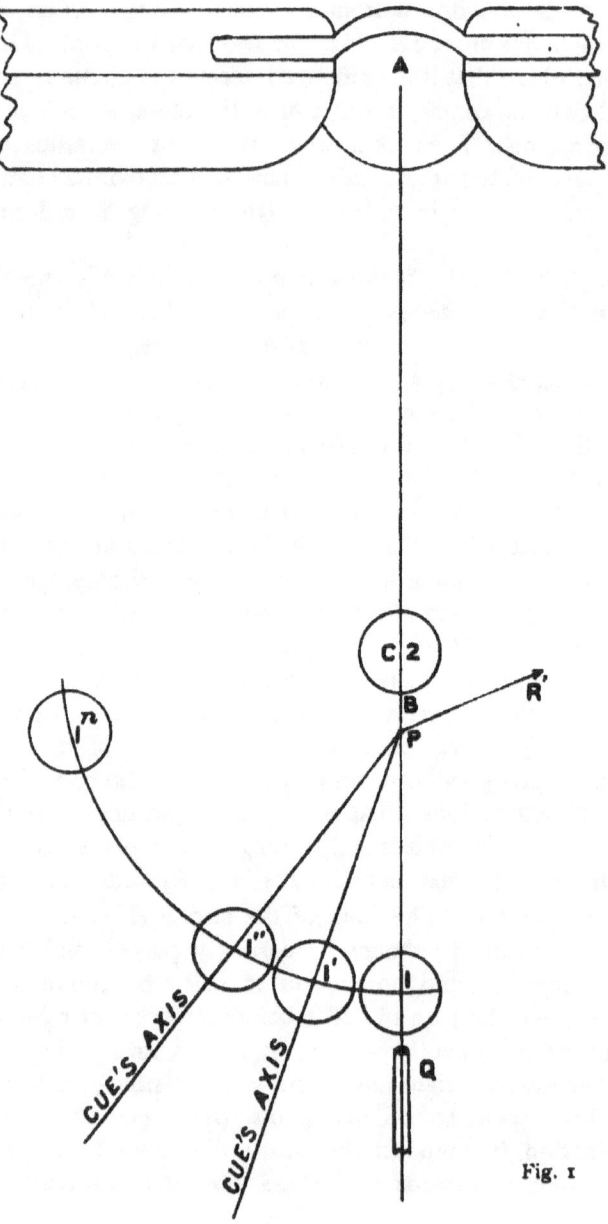

Fig. 1

THREE-BALL PRACTICE

pockets till a tolerable certainty or confidence is acquired. Some persons will make the full, whilst others will play the fine strokes best ; and again, it will often be found that, when playing into the right-hand pocket, there is a tendency to error on one or other side, but when playing to the left-hand pocket the mistake is just reversed. If the strokes are taken too full to the right, they will be made too fine to the left. The proper procedure is obvious : by making a very small allowance each way the mistake will be corrected, the eyes will become educated, and the tendency to error will diminish. It need scarcely be added that the kind of stroke in which one has least confidence should receive the most attention ; failure indicates where practice is required.

Also, let the path of ball 1, after impact, receive close attention, and as soon as some certainty in making the hazard is felt, let the exercise consist quite as much in playing to leave ball 1 in or near a desired place as in the success of the hazard. The value of this is all but self-evident, and it is as important in pool or pyramids as in billiards.

Similar practice may, with advantage, be made to the top corner pockets, ball 2 being placed on the billiard, and afterwards on the pyramid spot. The rules for finding what point of 2 should be struck and the points of aim are, of course, unaltered, but attention may usefully be given to the following hint, based on the construction of the cushions at the neck of the pocket. Whether a pocket is easy or not depends, perhaps, more on this than on the actual width at the fall. If the channel is gradually rounded off, with but little rubber in the sides, a ball once in the neck is nearly sure to fall into the pocket ; but if there is much rubber in the sides, the same ball would expend its energy in rebounding from side to side, and have no disposition to travel forward into the pocket. Cushions cut square, as it is called, make the pockets more difficult than those sloped gently away ; the channel is narrower.

Let ball 2 be placed between the spot and the top cushion, or anywhere on a line connecting a point so chosen and

the corner pocket into which it is proposed to play. In
this case the point of aim is no longer the true centre of the
pocket, nor even the centre of the portion of the pocket which
is open from position 2, but a point so chosen that ball 2 may
impinge on the neck or side of the pocket entrance, and
thence drop in. The accompanying sketch will show what is
meant. If ball 2 were played on C, the centre of the pocket,
it would strike the cushion A, and very probably rebound to
the opposite side, and the hazard would fail; but if, on the
contrary, it strike the cushion B at a point T, inside the neck

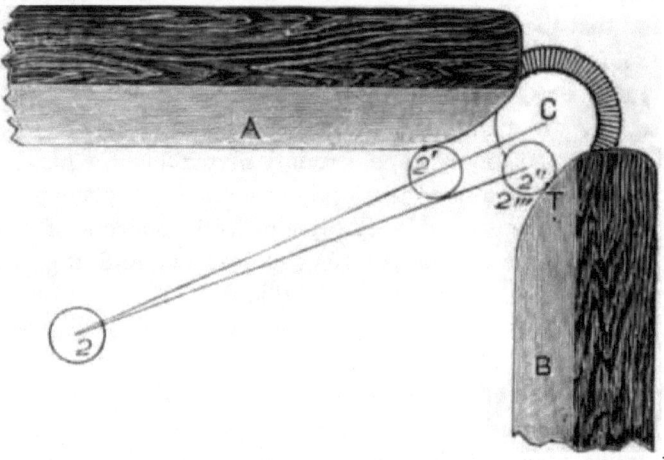

Fig. 2

of the pocket, then, unless played very hard, the hazard will
to a certainty be made.

With reference to the position of ball 2, C is termed a blind
pocket, because the full width at the fall is not open. Hazards
into blind pockets are therefore more difficult than those into
open ones; nevertheless, if the player is careful to observe the
required point of impact, and to allow accordingly in aim, such
strokes can be played with considerable confidence.

When measurements are given whereby the positions of
balls on the billiard-table may be found, they must not be
supposed to be absolutely accurate. They no doubt are nearly

THREE-BALL PRACTICE

so for the table and balls with which the stroke was played for the purposes of this volume; but tables, balls, cloth, and climate are subject to variation which may make modification necessary, and, moreover, each man has a mode of using his cue as peculiar to himself as is his handwriting. Therefore, once for all, let it be understood that the diagrams and descriptions must be treated as but approximate. All measurements from a cushion are from the edge on which balls impinge to the centre of the ball whose position is to be fixed; those from a pocket are from the middle of the fall. The dotted lines with figures marked in Diagram I., example A, show the measurements whereby the position of ball 2 is determined. Many mistakes are made by inaccurate reading of instructions, and by failure to use the measure correctly, but the eye will prove a useful check; for if the position of the balls, when placed on the table, does not nearly coincide with that shown in the diagram, there is an error somewhere which a little patience and consideration will cause to be discovered.

A few typical strokes are shown on Diagram I.:—

A. Ball 1, on or near the right corner of the **D**; ball 2 $7\frac{1}{2}$ in. below the right middle pocket, and 8 in. from cushion 3. The measurements are in this instance shown on the diagram as a guide in other cases.

Play a free No. 1 strength. Ball 1, after pocketing 2, should travel to the top cushion, and so far back as to leave an easy winning hazard on a ball on the billiard spot. With slight variation of the position, the stroke may be played slower or faster, as may be desired. If the strength is misjudged, and ball 1 should stop somewhere between the top cushion and the desired position, a losing hazard in the left top pocket may not improbably be possible. The positions of both balls may be considerably varied, whilst the stroke remains virtually unchanged. The further ball 1 is brought to the left along the baulk-line, the fuller is the hazard, and the position of ball 1 after the stroke will be more to the right of the spot than that shown in the diagram.

B. Ball 1, 25½ in. from cushion 2, and 15 in. from the top cushion.

Ball 2, touching the top cushion and 12 in. from the right top pocket. Play a gentle No. 1, which will leave ball 1 about 7 in. from cushion 2 and 14 in. from the top cushion.

In this stroke ball 2 and the cushion are simultaneously struck, as will be apparent if ball 1 be placed against ball 2 at the proper point of impact; hence a very common rule is to

Instead of Long Rest

direct the player to aim between ball and cushion. The general rule however for finding the point of impact holds good, and the fact that under the circumstances the cushion is struck at the same time as the ball is merely a coincidence.

C. Ball 1, 3 in. from the left side cushion, and 9 in. from the left top pocket.

Ball 2, touching the left side cushion and 4½ in. from left top pocket. Play a very soft stroke so that ball 1 may be left at 1'; a losing hazard from the spot is then open. This stroke

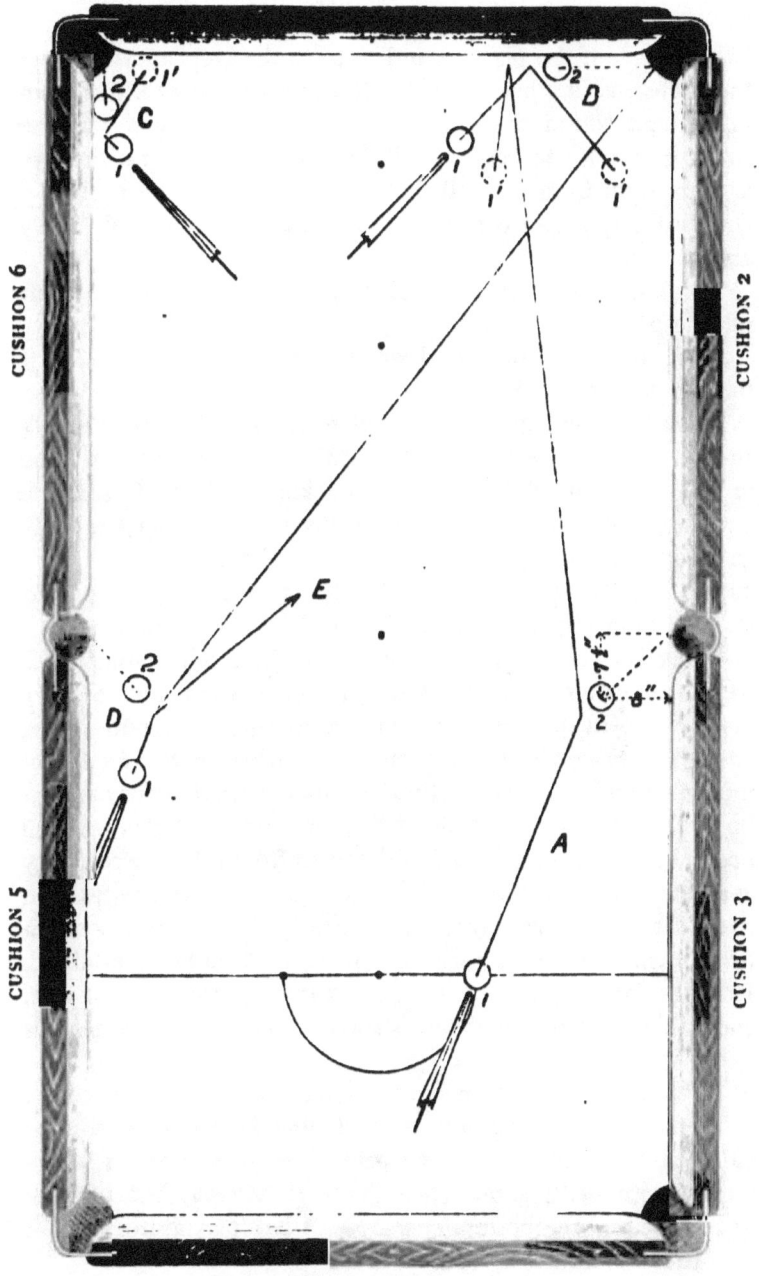

Diagram I.

is best made if the player stand close to the balls and lean over the table, making his bridge for the cue *bouclée—i.e.* the forefinger bent round the cue. If played in the usual way the stroke could not be reached without the long rest, and the eye is then so far from the ball that error and failure are probable. Any ordinary player can show the stroke, which is quite easy and very useful.

D. Ball 1, 5 in. from cushion 5 and 17 in. below the left middle pocket.

Ball 2, 6 in. from cushion 5 and 7 in. below the left middle pocket.

This is an example of a hazard to a blind pocket. Ball 1 should be struck gently, and its position after the stroke will be in the direction of the right top pocket. It is, in fact, a fine cut, and if played with sufficient strength ball 1 may probably go into the right top pocket. If ball 1 be placed 6 in. from cushion 5, the stroke is slightly fuller and may be played slower; after impact the ball will travel in the direction D E.

Diagram II. shows positions for doubles, with which it is well to accustom the eye. Though such strokes are not very much used in billiards, they are occasionally of great value, and their principle is based on the equality of the angles of incidence and reflexion. It is clear that a double may be set up at almost any part of the table, and it is well that several positions should be selected and played from till some certainty is obtained; those shown in the diagram are merely types. In these cases ball 1 is played full or nearly so on 2, and position for a further score may with attention to strength be attained. Doubles are used more in pool and pyramids than in billiards, and will be treated in detail when the two former games are described.

It may be as well to make a few remarks explanatory of the diagram. A is an example of a double in baulk where the balls are easily reached. The point A on the cushion where impact with ball 2 should take place is half-way between the baulk-line and the bottom cushion. A ball played from B to A

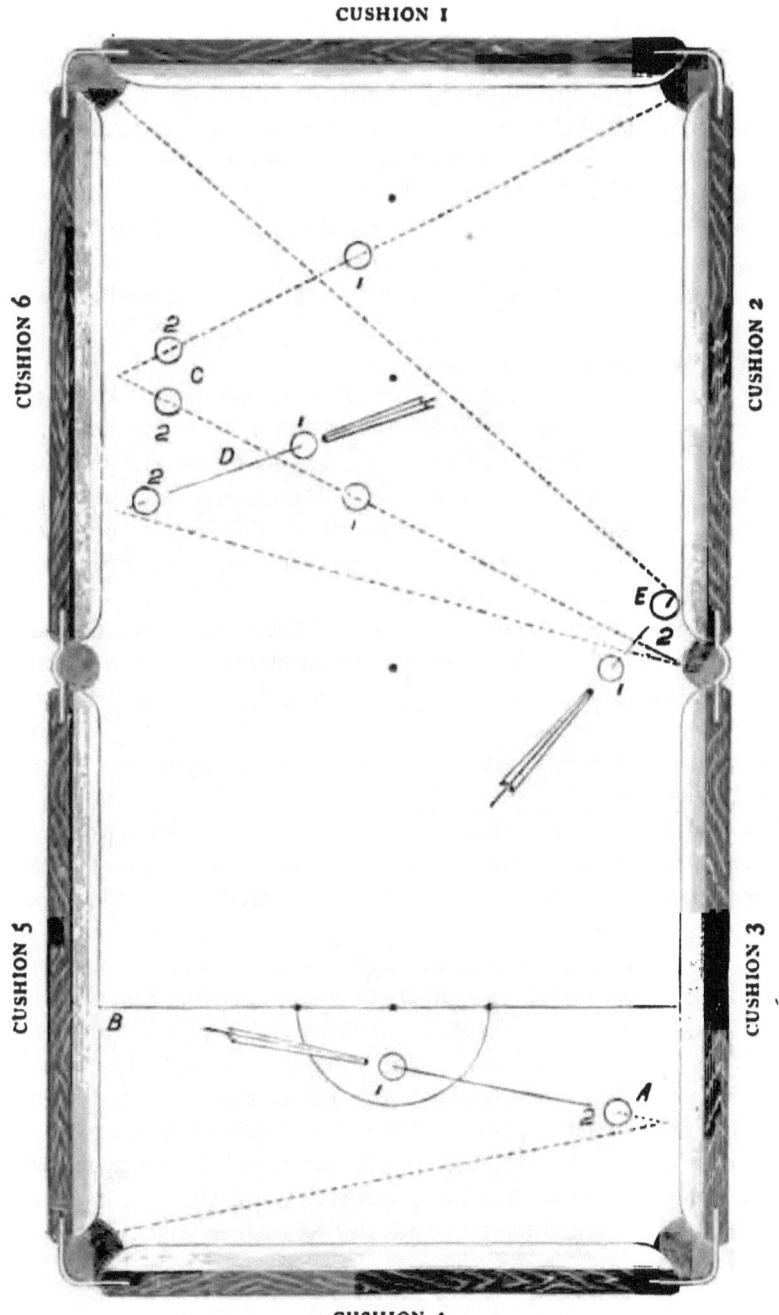

Diagram II.

should, if truly struck in the centre, fall into the left bottom pocket. Place balls 1 and 2 as shown in the diagram on the line B A, keeping 2 sufficiently far from the cushion to avoid a kiss ; play full, and 2 should be doubled. Again, let c be the middle point of cushion 6, and imagine lines joining it with the right middle and right top pockets. On these lines place the balls. A full stroke from ball 1 to 2 should double the latter in the one case into the right top pocket, in the other into the right middle pocket.

Next, D is an instance of a simple double, from which in more ways than one a losing hazard from spot may be left. Ball 1 is 24 in. from cushion 6 and $26\frac{1}{2}$ in. above the middle pocket; ball 2 is 5 in. from the same cushion and $20\frac{1}{2}$ in. above the pocket. A full stroke will double ball 2 into the right middle pocket, and ball 1 may be left near the line from the left middle pocket to the spot.

In the case marked E, ball 2 is just beyond the shoulder of the right middle pocket, ball 1 being so placed nearly in a line from 2 to the left bottom pocket that a full stroke about No. 1 strength will carry 2 to the left top pocket. Ball 1 may be so played as to leave a losing hazard into the left top pocket from a ball on spot.

All these strokes should be played medium strength, say No. 1 or 2 ; in practice it will be found that the angle of reflexion varies somewhat with the strength, and in a less degree with the table.

As great accuracy is of the highest importance in playing winning hazards, it is evident that, when either ball has a considerable distance to travel, the stroke should not be played too slowly ; for in a very slow stroke imperfections of ball or table tell more than when greater strength is used. Also, before leaving the subject, it is desirable to impress the reader strongly with the importance of the remarks on pages 145-6 respecting play into a more or less blind pocket. Attention to them is essential to good spot play and also to what is called play at

THREE-BALL PRACTICE

the top of the table. Clearing the dangerous shoulder of the pocket is the secret of success.

We now proceed to losing hazards, which with most amateurs form the mainstay of the game ; partly because being easier than winning hazards, they are usually taught first, but mainly because they are possible with a slovenly style and inaccurate striking which effectually prevent success with winners. In reality, however, they will repay care and accuracy as much as any other stroke, because, unless ball 2 be struck in the proper place, it will not travel in the desired path, and the result of a poor stroke may be success as regards the hazard, coupled with leaving ball 2 hopelessly safe. When played with intelligence and with due regard to the position of ball 2 after the stroke, they form most excellent practice. Following the usual custom, these strokes may be divided into short and long losers, and each will be separately treated ; at present, of course, plain strokes only being considered. It is convenient to take the half-ball hazard as the standard or typical stroke ; it is the easiest for the reason given at p. 133, because aim is taken at the edge of ball 2, a well-defined mark, instead of at an indefinite point on the ball's surface. Moreover, on billiard-tables certain positions are recognised as affording half-ball losers, and these are most valuable to a player as supplying the means, during play, of testing and correcting his strokes or his judgment of angles. It often happens from many causes that a man's eye or nerve partially fails, which failure destroys confidence and begets still worse play ; he probably before long gets a stroke from one of the many positions which should be played half-ball. The mere effort to recognise the situation tends to arrest demoralisation, whilst the success which follows correct recognition goes far to restore equanimity and confidence. That is one reason against wantonly altering the positions of the spots on the table, the size of the D and such matters ; though, no doubt, if the game can thereby be certainly improved, the alteration is justified, and in time players will learn similar positions under the altered circumstances. Hitherto such changes have been made rather with the view of cramping the play of one or two men, and so placing others less able or less diligent on a par with them, than with the object of making an undeniable improvement in the game. Such modifications under the pretext of reform are much to be deprecated.

Taking the billiard, pyramid, and centre spots as fixed points on the table, Diagram III. shows with sufficient accuracy the lines of half-ball strokes to the top pockets. Let the billiard spot be considered first. From either top pocket there is a half-ball stroke to the opposite one; also from either middle pocket there is similarly a half-ball hazard into the opposite top pocket. Next, from a ball placed on the pyramid spot there are half-ball hazards from either corner of the D into the top pockets; and, lastly, from a ball on the centre spot, half-ball strokes to either top pocket may be made from positions about $7\frac{1}{2}$ in. to the right and left of the centre spot of baulk. Precise accuracy in definition of these strokes is not attempted; tables and balls vary, whilst no two men strike exactly alike; hence each must work out for himself the exact position for a half-ball stroke; it will in every case be reasonably near the lines indicated.

Diagram IV. illustrates several losing hazards, all good for practice. For the group marked A, place ball 1 on an imaginary line from the centre of the red spot to the upper edge of the shoulder of the left middle pocket about half-way between them, where it can be conveniently reached by the player; it is then in position for a gentle half-ball stroke to the right top pocket. When correctly played, impact with ball 2 takes place on the central longitudinal line of the table, and consequently 2 travels to the top cushion on that line, and returns on the same path a shorter or greater distance according to the strength of stroke. A very gentle one will bring ball 2 back to the spot; a medium stroke will result in leaving it near the pyramid spot, and it can be brought further down the table if desired; but for practice at this stage endeavour should be made to leave ball 2 between the red and pyramid spots on the centre line. If this is effected, ball 2 has been truly struck; should it return to the right of

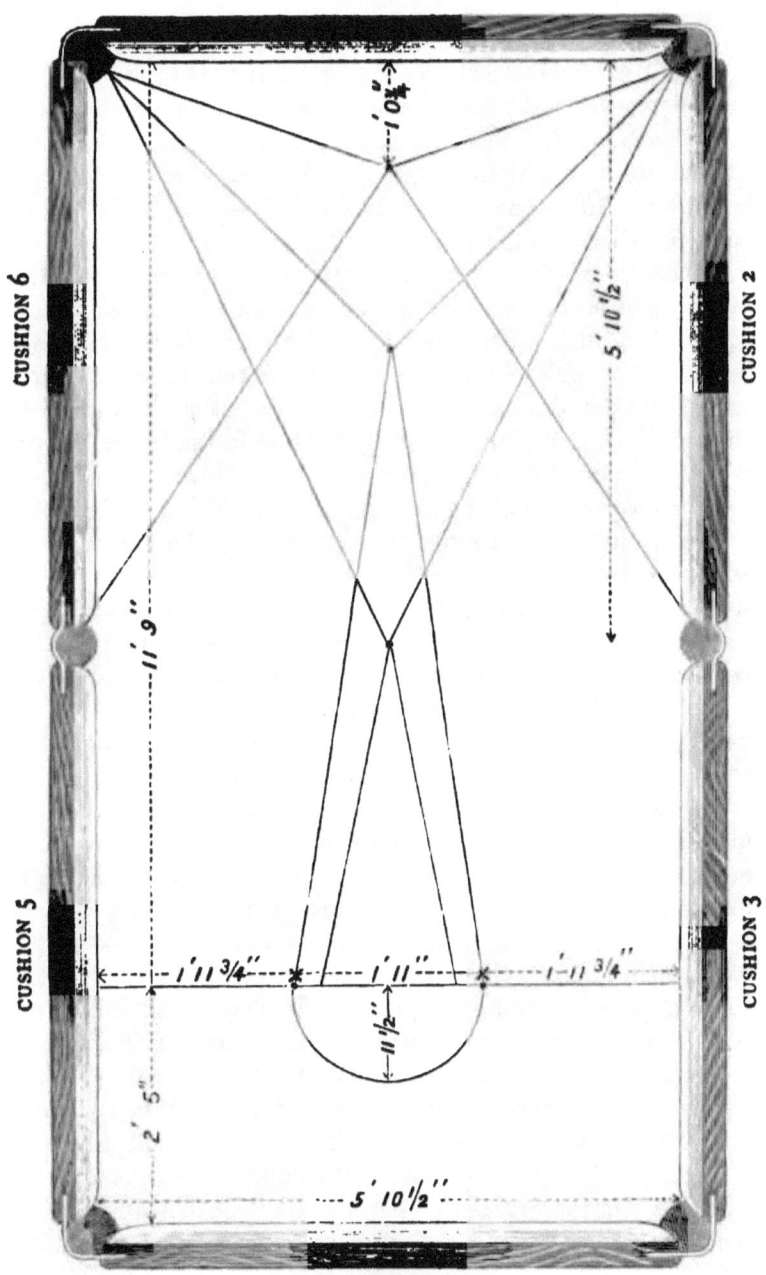

Diagram III.

the line it has been struck too full, and if it rests to the left of the line too fine. So that here again we have an index which points out error and shows what is required for its correction. The hazard is so easy that after a little practice it will seldom be missed, and for that reason it should be worked at till it becomes what is called a certainty.

Then from A lay off, in the direction of the right middle pocket, a series of positions marked A' A'' A''' A'''', each about $1\frac{3}{4}$ in. from the other, and from each of these play the hazard. The point of impact should be the same in every case, therefore the point of aim will vary slightly with the change of position; but the chief variation in the stroke lies in the strength employed.

For the position A' the strength is about No. 2, and ball 2 should be left on the central line L L between the centre spot and the bottom cushion. For A'' the same stroke a little stronger, ball 2 returning from the bottom cushion towards the centre spot: and so on. It is seldom necessary to practise beyond A''' in dealing with plain strokes. The strength required for this stroke is considerable approaching No. 4, and ball 2 should travel beyond twice the length of the table. In all these strokes endeavour should be made to keep ball 2 travelling on the line L L; this will be found not quite an easy matter, and sometimes divergence may not be from any fault of striking, for an imperfection in the ball which might account for an error of half an inch or less in 6 ft. would produce a perceptible deviation during a journey of 24 to 30 ft. Nevertheless, the prime source of failure is to be looked for in a faulty method on the part of the player, who, if he cannot easily remedy what is wrong, should without hesitation revert to the practice previously prescribed. After some work at this he will probably find that ball 1 was not being truly struck, and will amend the fault. These strokes should then be transferred to the other side of the table, making the hazards into the left top pocket. They are very conveniently played with the left hand, and the player who can use both hands

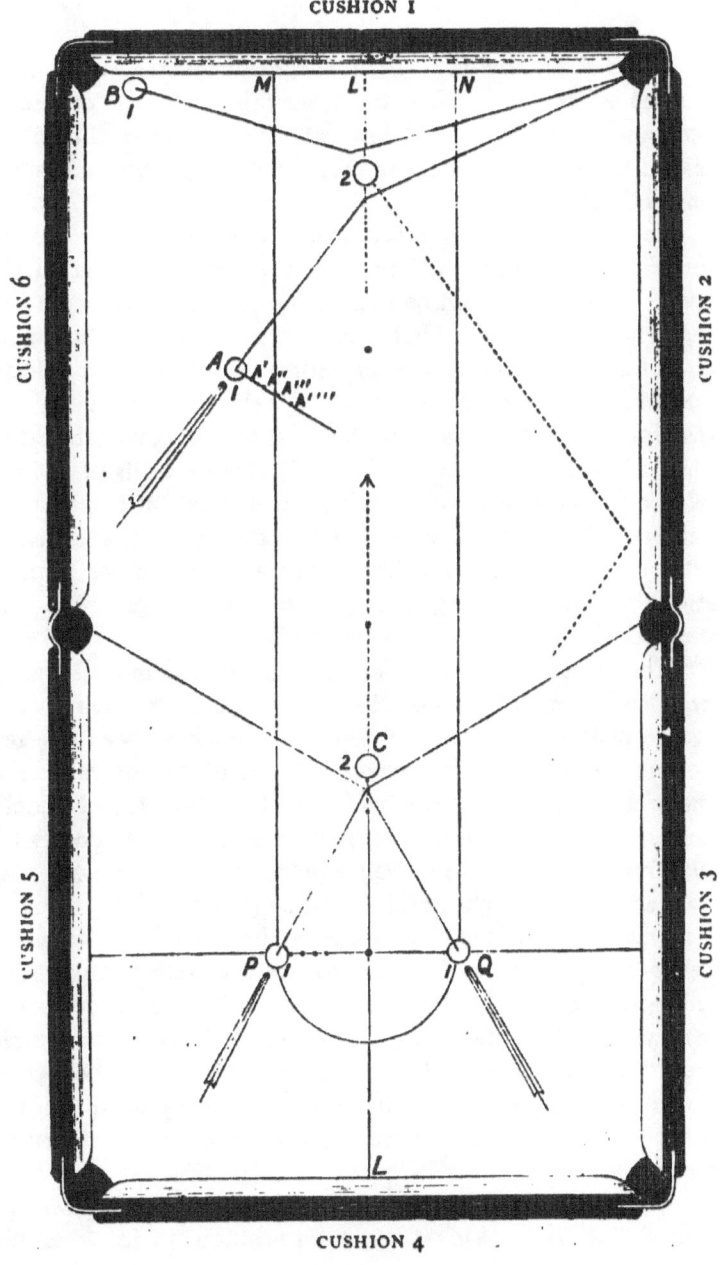

Diagram IV.

almost indifferently has a great advantage over a purely one-handed performer. It is entirely, we think, a matter of resolution and of practice. At any rate, these strokes should be played from both sides of the table till they can be made without difficulty.

Example B exhibits a valuable stroke of common occurrence. Ball 1 is on the line from the left top pocket to the spot. That line should be taken from a point nearer the top than the side cushion. Ball 2 should be struck so as to drive it as indicated, half a foot or more above the right middle pocket on to the cushion, whence it rebounds and comes to rest conveniently over that pocket. A similar stroke should be played from the right top pocket, and there is as usual a little license as to the position of ball 1; it may be further from or nearer to the pocket than is shown in the diagram, and also a little above or below the line indicated, and still be a plain stroke; when the divergence is greater, side is required, and the methods of play will be hereafter explained.

The strokes marked C on this diagram afford admirable practice for middle pocket losing hazards; for their results record plainly the errors committed. They have been selected because the point of impact on ball 2 is in the central line of the table; therefore, as has been already shown, its path should lie on that line. Another advantage these strokes possess is that from each position of ball 2 precisely similar hazards may be made into the right and left middle pocket.

Place ball 2 in the central line of the table, 24 in. from the baulk-line. A half-ball hazard is open from either the right or left corner of the D. Ball 2 should pass up and down the central line, the distance varying with the strength; for simple hazard practice it should be brought back to its place before the stroke was made. Next bring ball 2 $1\frac{1}{2}$ in. down the central line; place ball 1 10 in. from the centre of baulk; play as before.

This stroke may be repeated by bringing ball 2 down the central line $1\frac{1}{2}$ in. each time, till a position 18 in. from the

THREE-BALL PRACTICE

baulk-line is reached. When nearer than this the stroke is so far changed that the strength must be reduced, so that ball 2 shall not return from the top cushion, but shall be cut towards one of the top pockets, and as the position of ball 2 approaches the baulk-line it will be found desirable to place ball 1 further and further back in the baulk within the limits of the **D**. Ball 1 is placed $1\frac{1}{2}$ in. towards the centre for each stroke up to the fifth when ball 2 is 18 in. from baulk. Whilst accuracy should be aimed at, its perfect attainment is impossible; in playing these strokes occasionally a very good one may be made, and ball 2 may keep very close to the central line. Oftener, however, there will be divergence, and hence it is well to recognise limits within which the stroke, though not very good, may yet suffice to leave ball 2 in play. In the diagram the lines P M and Q N, drawn from the corners of the **D** parallel to the sides of the table, form such boundaries. If ball 2 be left anywhere in the space so inclosed, and as far down the table as the spot, there is almost certainly a plain hazard to be made off it from baulk into either top or middle pockets.

Other and easier middle pocket hazards may be indefinitely multiplied, and should be practised till the person playing acquires confidence, not merely that he can make the stroke, but that he can vary the strength at will from such delicacy as scarcely to move ball 2 to one which will bring it in and out of baulk. A few examples are given in Diagram V.

A. Ball 2, $16\frac{1}{2}$ in. from cushion 3, $12\frac{1}{2}$ in. below right middle pocket; ball 1 on right corner of the **D**. Play half-ball about No. 2 strength, leaving ball 2 placed for a hazard in the left middle pocket. Ball 2 can be brought back nearly over the centre spot, and the danger of the stroke is that, if played too fine, ball 2 will lie near cushion 6 and be practically out of play.

B. Ball 2, $15\frac{1}{2}$ in. from cushion 3, 6 in. below right middle pocket; ball 1 on baulk centre spot. Play half-ball No. 2 strength, leaving ball 2 with hazard into right middle pocket.

C. Ball 2, 21 in. from cushion 5, 10 in. below left middle pocket; ball 1 on baulk centre spot. Play half-ball No. 2 strength, bringing ball 2 back over or near the centre spot of the table. With slight variation of strength and aim ball 2 can be brought back into almost any desired position on the table.

D. Ball 2, 9 in. from cushion 5, 23½ in. below left middle pocket; ball 1, 5½ in. to the right of the centre of baulk, or on position 5 of Example C, Diagram IV. Play a half-ball slow No. 1. Ball 2 will travel to the side cushion on a line at right angles to its face, or, in other words, parallel to the baulk-line, and will return on the same line to a distance varying with the strength. A medium No. 1 strength will bring the ball back from 24 to 30 in. from the side cushion. There is great latitude in placing ball 1 for this stroke, which can be made as far as 8½ in. to the right of baulk centre, the difference in play being merely in strength. The further ball 1 is placed from 2 the greater is the strength required, and as a consequence the further does ball 2 return from the side cushion. This stroke is of the class called 'jennies.' Each stroke here recommended for practice can be played from either side of the table; and this should always be done in order that the eye may become equally familiar with the angles into either side pocket.

The next two examples (Diagram VI.) are of an importance which the beginner may not at once realise, but which is abundantly clear to a professional or to an advanced amateur. The hazards are in themselves so easy that a very poor player can have no difficulty in making them; but mark the difference between the right and wrong method of play. In the first example the paths of ball 2 after impact are drawn, both when rightly and when wrongly struck; and an examination of them will show that if the proper method is followed, error in strength has much less effect in leaving the ball out of play, and if the stroke is wrongly played the margin for such error is comparatively small. The principle here illustrated

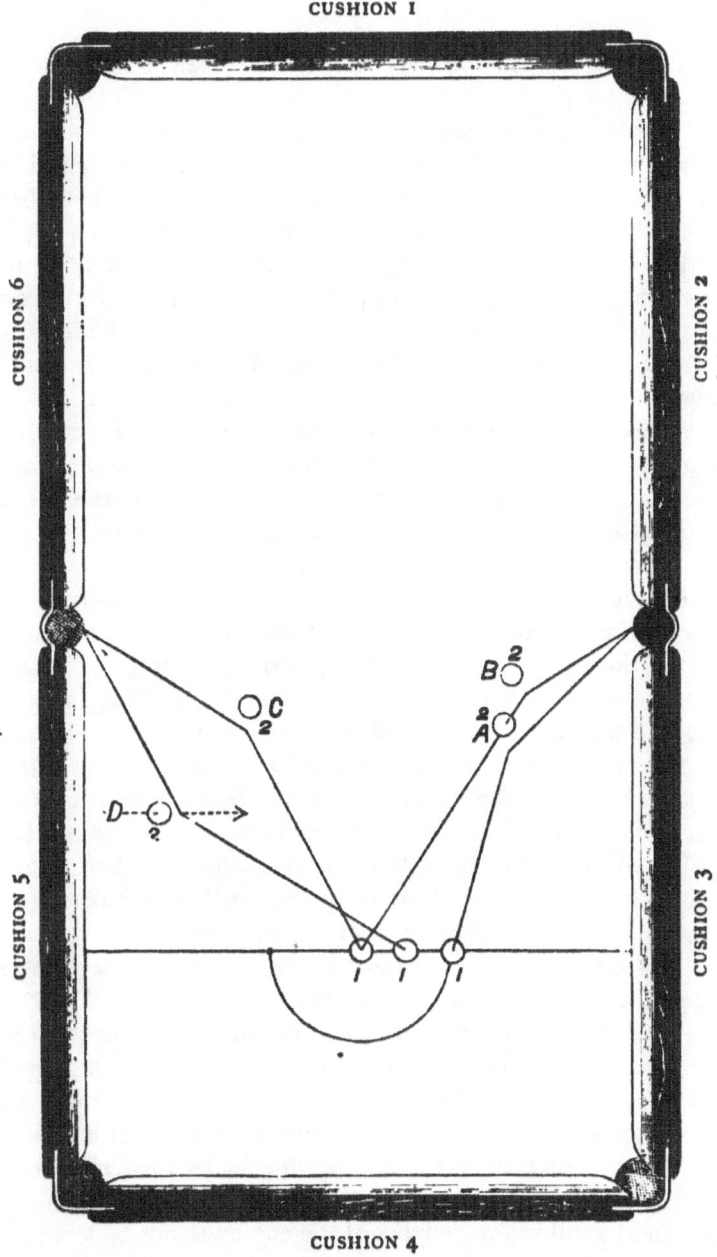

Diagram V.

applies to many positions, and consequently the strokes deserve close study.

Example A.—Place ball 1, 40 in. from the top cushion, 7 in. from cushion 6; ball 2, 16 in. from the top cushion, 11 in. from cushion 6; play a free stroke rather finer than half-ball; it is a bad stroke indeed which leaves ball 2 out of play. Another good example is shown at B; ball 1, 24 in. from cushion 4, 4½ in. from cushion 3; ball 2, 13 in. from cushion 4, 9 in. from cushion 3. Play a free stroke finer than half-ball on 2, which will follow a course somewhat resembling that indicated.

Diagram VII. may be thus set up :—Ball 2, 5 in. from left middle pocket, ½ in. above a line joining the centres of the two middle pockets; place ball 1 7 in. to the right of the centre spot in baulk; play half-ball on ball 2 a free stroke. Ball 2 must be very badly struck if it is left out of play; it should strike the left side and top cushions and return to position. If played improperly, it returns from the top cushion only, and unless the strength is very exact is probably lost to play. Many accidents may happen; it may be holed in the left top pocket, or, still worse, catch in it and run safe under the top cushion; it may return close to cushion 6 and come to rest either above or below the middle pocket; in each case it is left in a more or less undesirable position. If played too full, ball 2 will probably be left safe near cushion 2; hence there are at least two types of wrong paths which might be shown, but they have been omitted to avoid complicating the diagram.

Having fairly mastered short losing hazards, the next step is to study similar strokes into the top pockets from baulk. They are called long losing hazards, and form an excellent test of a performer's capacity at the game of billiards, in which they fill an important part. They require greater accuracy than the short hazards, because the balls have to travel over a greater distance, so that correctness in placing ball 1 for a plain half-ball stroke on ball 2 is of the greatest consequence. Smoothness and truth in the delivery of the cue must not be lost sight

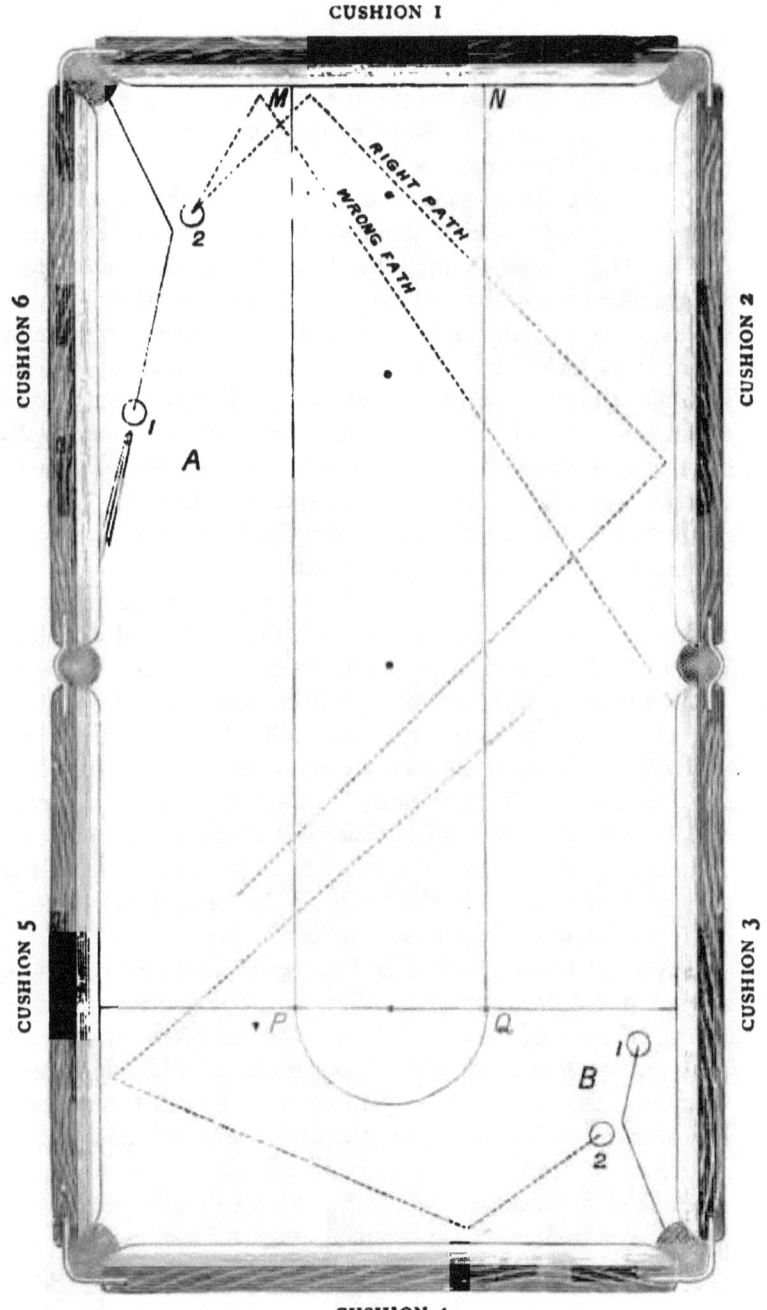

Diagram VI.

of, and a short reversion to the practice recommended in Chapters III. and IV. for the attainment of these objects will prove to be of much benefit.

The typical long losing hazard is made from ball 2 on the centre spot, ball 1 being about $7\frac{1}{2}$ in. from the centre of the baulk. Differences in the elasticity of the balls will make a slight alteration in the best position for ball 1 ; where it is considerable, 8 in. may not be too far from baulk spot, and where it is less 7 in. will suffice ; the position also varies with the strength of stroke. This hazard is rightly considered a difficult one, and it cannot be mastered without much application ; it is indeed now of more value than of old, because in a break when ball 1 is left touching another ball, the game is continued by placing the adversary's ball on the centre spot, the red on spot, and playing from baulk.

The stroke can be made with considerable difference of strength, which varies of course with the position desired for ball 2. Ball 1 should be struck in the centre (not below) about No. 2 strength ; this will bring ball 2 back over the middle pocket, the stroke being played half-ball. If it be made ten or twelve times in succession on a clean table, the path travelled by 1 after impact will be fairly visible, and it is an instructive subject of study. First there is a straight line to within the length of a radius of the point of impact, next there is a somewhat violent curve, the result of the forward course suddenly modified by impact, the rebound due to elasticity and the frictional action between ball and cloth, and this in turn is merged into a second straight line. The action described is not peculiar to this stroke, but is visible in many others, and exists more or less in all, but this one forms a favourable opportunity for observation. The path travelled by ball 1 is roughly indicated in fig. 3, and the practical lesson to be learned therefrom is that in playing cannons the curve must never be overlooked or forgotten when the third ball lies within the sphere of its influence. Reference has just been made to the impact of two balls and the rebound which follows, a subject

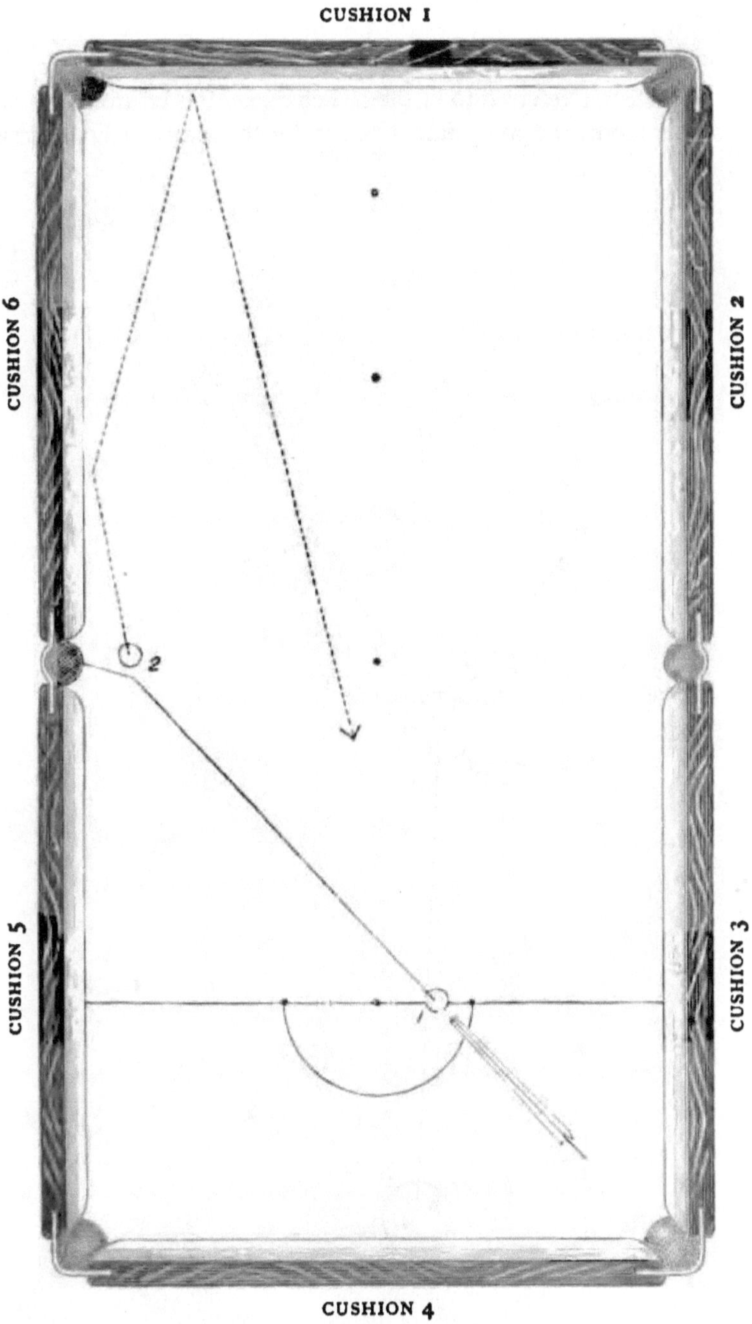

CUSHION 1

CUSHION 6

CUSHION 2

CUSHION 5

CUSHION 3

CUSHION 4

Diagram VII.

67

which was referred to in the last chapter ; it is of interest, and at this moment appropriate, to consider the matter a little further.

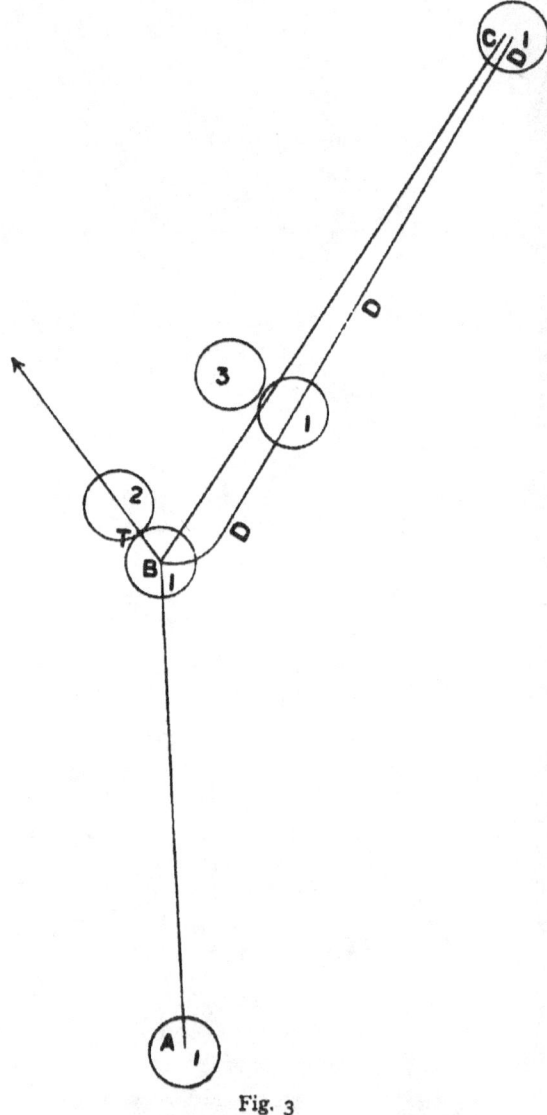

Fig. 3

THREE-BALL PRACTICE

In fig. 3 ball 1 played on 2 impinges at T; 2 travels from T as shown by the arrow. B C shows the line travelled by 1 after impact as it is exhibited in the diagrams; but the true path is more nearly B D. Hence it is clear that a cannon on ball 3 would just be missed, the position of 1 being indicated in the act of passing 3. The tendency of the lines B D and B C to approach each other and ultimately to coincide is apparent. It is also clear that the magnitude of the curve B D depends on the strength of stroke as well as on the elasticity of the balls. If played very hard, it will be greater; if very soft, it will almost disappear, the line of travel approximating to B C, in which case it is evident the cannon would be made.

The balls may for our purpose be assumed to be of equal density and perfectly elastic; that is, they are equally hard, equally heavy, and when they receive the shock of impact they recover their figure or shape with a force equal to that which caused the momentary compression. What happens more or less in every stroke in which one ball is made to strike another is that at the moment of collision the round surfaces are flattened by the shock, and impact is not confined to what is accurately called a point, but is extended to this flattened surface, which varies in size according to the strength of the stroke, the hardness of the balls, and the part of ball 2 struck. In using a very perfect set of ivory balls $2\frac{3}{32}$ in. diameter, in a stroke rather fuller than half-ball with strength from No. 3 to 4, this temporary flattening was found to extend to about the size of the head of a small tin-tack, say $\frac{1}{10}$ in. in diameter; nearly but not quite as large as the billiard balls shown in the diagrams. The rebound is due to the reaction whereby the balls recover their normal shape; in the case of ball 2, which was at rest before impact, the effect is to make it travel on a line from the point of impact through its centre; the effect on ball 1, which was not only moving forward but also revolving, being to check its velocity, some of which is imparted to ball 2, to rebound, and to assume a new path, the first part of which is curved as a result of the blending of the various forces to which it is subjected. In this explanation no pretence to a mathematical solution is made; it is simply the result of watching the behaviour of the balls and endeavouring to account for it by an exercise of common-sense. Most persons who have played much must have noticed occasional stains of red on the white ball; these were the results of impact, and if carefully examined would be found to be small circular spots; similarly all persons are familiar with the fact that the red ball gradually loses its colour, which it parts with in the way here noticed.

Now to return to the long losing hazards; the usual mistake is to place ball 1 for a stroke finer than half-ball, the result being that it strikes the side cushion on the dangerous shoulder; therefore, when in doubt, allow for this and place the ball for a full rather than for a fine stroke. The hazard from ball 2 on the central point of the table should be constantly practised, first into one top pocket and next into the other, till it can be made with considerable facility and with varied strength. Then let ball 2 be placed on the pyramid spot and ball 1 on or near the corner of the D; a half-ball stroke will make the losing hazard into either top pocket. Care should be taken not to hit ball 1 above the centre, and the strength should be about a soft No. 2. Ball 2, after striking the top and side cushions, should come to rest so that a middle pocket hazard may be left.

Between these two hazards a number of others may be interpolated, the most satisfactory plan being to set ball 2 at intervals of 6 in. from the centre spot up the central line towards the pyramid spot as shown in Diagram VIII. By this means six separate hazards are provided for practice, or four are inserted between the two already described. Taking these four 6 in. in succession above the centre spot; for the first, ball 1 should be placed about 7 in. from baulk centre; for the second about 5 in.; for the third about $2\frac{1}{2}$ in.; and for the fourth on the centre spot of the baulk. As before explained, these positions for ball 1 are but approximate; they require modification proportioned to the elasticity of the balls,

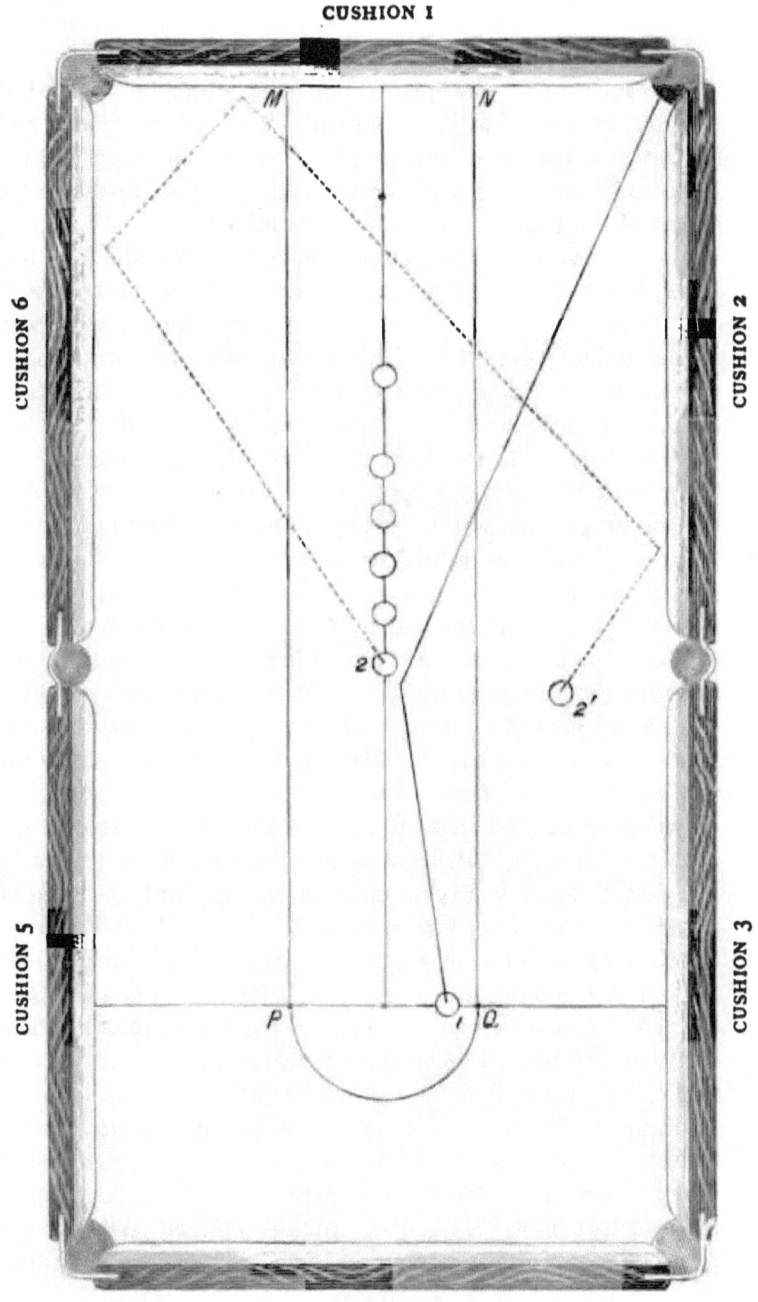

Diagram VIII.

the personality of the player, and the strength used. For example, from the position when ball 2 is on the centre spot and for the next two positions, in playing with bonzoline balls it would be prudent to place ball 1 from $\frac{1}{2}$ to $\frac{1}{4}$ in. further from centre of the D than the positions indicated.

When the eye has become acquainted with the half-ball angle, ball 2 should be set up anywhere within the lines P M, Q N (Diagram IX.), between the centre and billiard spots, and practice continued. Unless for some special purpose, endeavour should be made to leave ball 2 within the space inclosed by these lines.

On Diagram X. two hazards, when ball 2 is further up the table than the pyramid spot, are shown. They are types of two classes, either soft or strong strokes—forcing hazards, as they are called. A is of the latter class; that is, though the hazard can be played quite gently by the use of side, yet as a plain stroke from the left corner of the D the strength required would be such as to make it probable that ball 2 would be left in baulk after the stroke. To avoid this, place ball 1 so that the hazard may be played with strength sufficient to bring ball 2 in and out of baulk. Place ball 2 about 16 in. from the top cushion, and 26 in. from cushion 2; ball 1 should be played from baulk 8 in. to the left of the centre, a free No. 2 or No. 3 strength. Ball 2 will travel somewhat as shown by the dotted line; if struck fuller it will go further and keep better within the lines P M, Q N.

B is an example of a gentle stroke, and of a type which frequently occurs in the course of a game. Ball 2, 4 in. from the left side cushion and 4 in. from the top cushion. Place ball 1 on the baulk line on the left corner of the D. Play on to the left top cushion so as to rebound on 2 about half-ball. As in most other strokes, there is considerable latitude both as regards strength and the fulness or fineness with which ball 2 may be struck. A few trials will show where it is desirable to place ball 1 if a very gentle stroke is required, and where it should be put if a stronger one is wanted. That the latitude

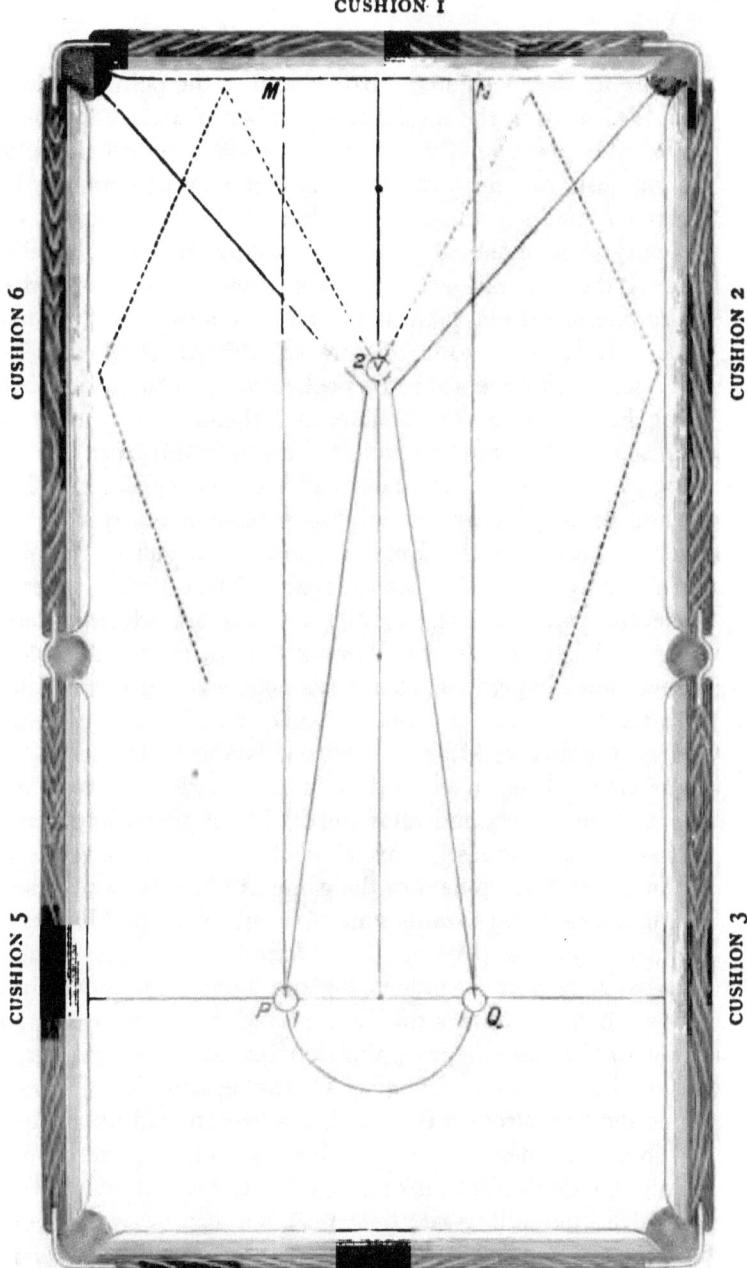

Diagram IX.

both as to the position of ball 2 and to the point of aim is great is clear from the results of a number of trials, ball 1 being played at a point on the left side cushion about 18 in. below the top cushion ; the path taken by ball 2 varied generally between the two shown on the diagram ; when it was struck full or nearly so, it impinged on the top cushion at R, and travelled towards the pyramid spot, and sometimes beyond it ; when struck fine it was cut towards M, and of course did not travel so far. It is useful to be able to play this stroke when ball 2 is at some distance from the pocket until, in fact, the direct losing hazard becomes possible, and therefore it should be practised till the eye can select with tolerable accuracy the point of the cushion at which ball 1 should be aimed. This method of playing by first striking a cushion or *bricole* is too much neglected in the English game, which suffers thereby ; when played it is often considered a fancy stroke, whereas numerous plain strokes, specially cannons, are advantageously made by its judicious use. Seeing that play from a cushion is sometimes imperative, as, for example, when player's ball is in hand and a certainty left in baulk, *bricole* practice from a variety of positions will well repay the labour bestowed.

What has been mentioned about the elasticity of balls and the consequent rebound after impact has a special importance in treating of cannons. This class of strokes has a tendency in the recent development of the game of billiards to supersede in a measure losing hazards which formerly, without doubt, were the mainstay of our players. The inferiority of losing to winning hazards in respect to influencing the game was conclusively shown when the spot stroke was played, but that stroke was rarely formidable save in professional hands ; the amateur, as might be expected, clinging to the easier losing hazard. When the spot stroke was barred, a substitute had to be found, and in a great measure this has been supplied by the cannon, chiefly, no doubt, in runs or series of strokes called nurseries (of which more will be said hereafter), but also by strokes which have the result of leaving the three balls close together, *gathering*

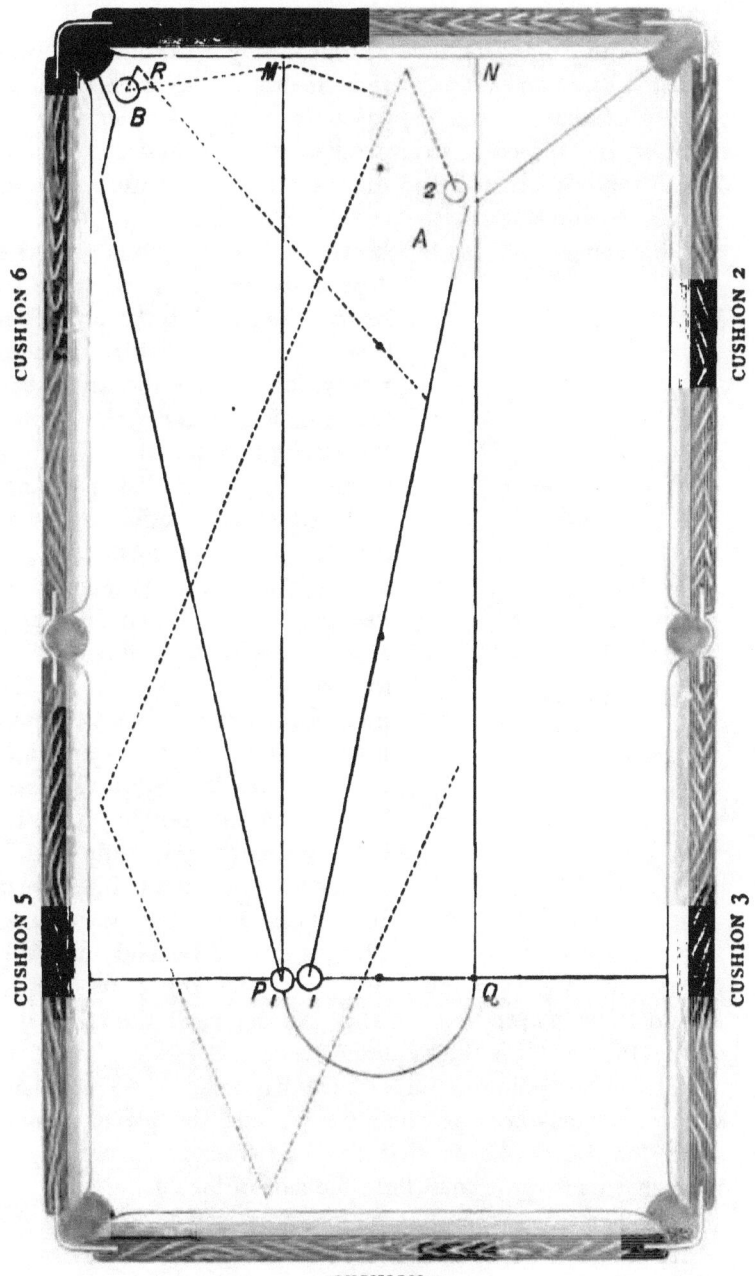

Diagram X.

them, as the Americans say. To deal fully with these involves the use of side and of other refinements of play with which as yet the student is not supposed to be familiar; at present attention is confined to plain strokes, which include those made direct from ball to ball and those made after impact with one or more cushions, but all played without side.

The general rule to be observed as to strength is to make it proportional to the distance to be traversed and to the angle between the paths of ball 1. That is to say, the smaller the angle between balls 1, 2, and 3, the greater the strength required. Figure 4 shows at a glance what is meant. Ball 1, played half-ball on 2, cannons on 3, as indicated by the lines. The nearer 3 approaches the position 3', which is nearly at right angles to a line joining the centres of 1 and 2, the harder must the stroke be played. When it passes the right angle and approaches to 3", screw is required in addition to strength; that is, ball 1, though still truly struck in its vertical central line, must be struck below its true centre. Hence it may be said that, the greater the angle or the finer the stroke, the more gently should it be played; the smaller the angle, or the fuller the stroke, the greater is the required strength.

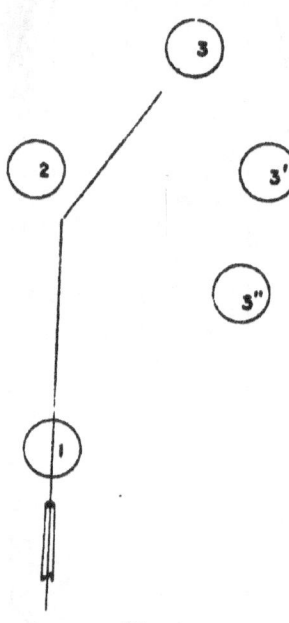

Fig. 4

The other point of importance is common to all plain strokes, but may here be usefully repeated; the player should stand for the stroke so that the line from 1 to 2 prolonged through 1 backwards shall form the axis of his cue..

Another matter never to be forgotten is that the finer the

THREE-BALL PRACTICE

stroke the less velocity ball 1 loses, and consequently the less is imparted to ball 2; the fuller the stroke the more 1 loses and 2 gains.

It is evident that, in every instance given of losing hazards, if ball 3 be substituted for the pocket the stroke will be converted from a hazard to a cannon; indeed, if that ball lie on any part of the path of ball 1 after impact or within the distance of a radius ($1\frac{1}{32}$ in.) on either side of the path, a cannon must result. Hence the examples for losing hazards are equally available for practice cannons, the eye-training for the requisite angle being the same. The cannon is in fact easier than the hazard, the target being nearly equal to the width of two balls, as fig. 5 shows; 1 played on 2 may just touch 3 to the left, when it would occupy the position 1′, or it may just touch the other side as shown, 1″. The width of this target varies with the distance between balls 2 and 3; at greatest it may be taken as double the size of a ball, or $4\frac{1}{8}$ in. The pocket on the other hand is usually $3\frac{5}{8}$ in. at the fall, the target it presents being under the most advantageous circumstances somewhat larger; on the other hand, when it is blind the target is reduced.

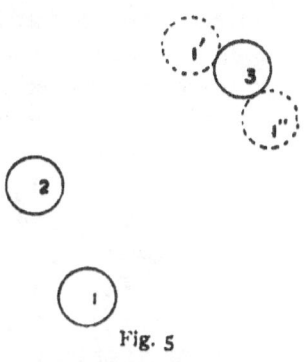

Fig. 5

A few cannons useful for practice, which if properly played result in gathering the balls, that is in leaving the three balls together, or so placing them that another stroke is left, are shown in the accompanying diagrams. In every case when indication is desirable the path of ball 1 is marked by a thin line; that of ball 2 by a dotted line; and that of ball 3 by a line consisting of a dash and dot alternately. In some cases the positions of the balls after the stroke are indicated thus:—1′, 2′, 3′; 1′ being the position which 1 has taken, and so on; in other cases this is not done because the situations are somewhat indeterminate, and also when the balls are but slightly moved the diagram would be confused and needlessly complicated.

The cannon shown in Diagram XI. is not merely an excellent plain stroke for practice, but the position is not infrequently met with or played for in a game, and is of a type which will repay close attention. As in all other cases, the measurements are merely approximate, and it is evident that a great variety of similar cannons can be set up simply by varying the position of ball 2. For ball 3 is supposed to be on the spot, and ball 1 in hand, so that a slight change in the position of ball 2, either up or down the table or in its distance from the side cushion, merely entails a corresponding move of ball 1, so that the cannon on ball 3 may always be played a soft half-ball. In the present instance, ball 2 is 18 in. from cushion 6, and $6\frac{1}{2}$ in. above the central transverse line of the table. If ball 1 be placed a little to the left of the baulk centre, say from 1 to 2 in., and played half-ball, so as to do little more than reach ball 3, and cannon on its right side, ball 2 will be brought towards the spot from which ball 3 has not been far removed. The balls may not improbably be left in the positions 1', 2', 3', in which case there is an excellent opening; but it must not be expected that in every instance fortune will be equally favourable. Still, unless the stroke is very badly played, the three balls will be left not far from each other, and at the top of the table, and that is a sufficient recommendation. The stroke, when correctly set up, simply requires a true half-ball plain stroke, with attention to strength. If ball 3 is sometimes hit on one side, sometimes on the other, and occasionally missed altogether, the inference is that accuracy in the half-ball stroke is wanting, and it is well to try and recover that by the methods previously recommended; when confidence is restored, then pay particular attention to the strength. Do not be satisfied till ball 3 is displaced from the spot not more than a few inches, say under six. Hence, in this class of cannons, which, like all other strokes, should, whenever possible, be practised under professional supervision, the first

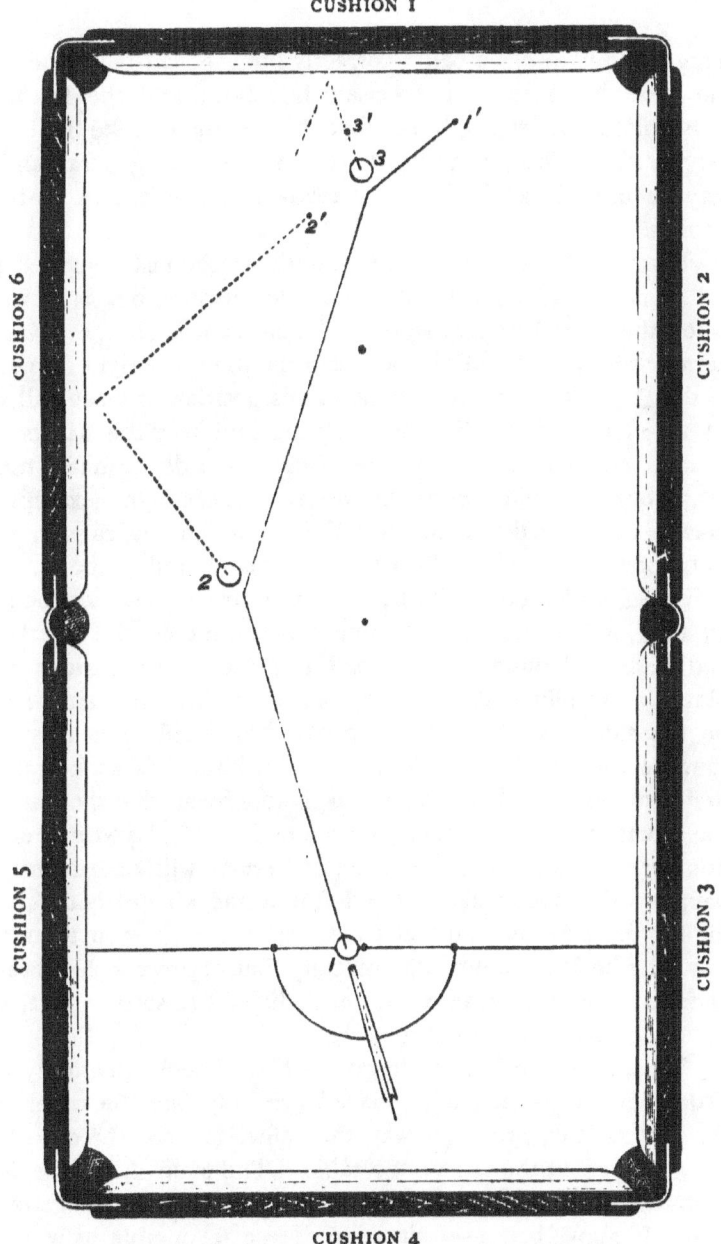

Diagram XI.

thing to do is to place ball 1 correctly for the half-ball angle; the next is to strike 2 precisely half-ball; and the last is to regulate the strength so that ball 1 shall strike ball 2 very gently. These remarks are to some extent general, and may be usefully applied, at the reader's discretion, to many strokes.

Diagram XII. shows a variation of the stroke just described; ball 2 is still 18 in. from the left side cushion, but is 3 in. below the central transverse line. There is, it is clear, a losing hazard into the left middle pocket from about the right corner of the **D**; but it is a better game in this position to place ball 1 $2\frac{1}{2}$ to $2\frac{3}{4}$ in. left of the baulk centre, and play the half-ball cannon. If ball 2 were further from the side cushion, the losing hazard would become the better stroke, and this example may be considered as almost the limit at which the cannon is to be preferred. The balls will approximately follow the paths indicated, and their positions after the stroke may be about 1', 2', 3', a fair chance remaining for continuing the break; and if, as will often happen, ball 1, placed a little wider or played a little finer, should strike ball 3 on the other side, *i.e.* on the side next the left top pocket, then ball 3 is driven towards the right top pocket, leaving a hazard (a winner for preference) into it, ball 2 is left, as before, near the spot, and the situation is still eminently favourable. If played a great number of times, some unfortunate results will occasionally happen; the three balls may be left in a line, all nearly touching the top cushion, and ball 1 between 2 and 3; even then a way may be found out of the difficulty, but at present the plain cannon is being considered, and it is difficult to set up on the table a better practice stroke.

The cannon shown in Diagram XIII., though apparently a little different, is, in reality, played precisely like the others; the results, too, are in a way the same, for the three balls are gathered at the top of the table. The main difference is that, the cannon being made off the top cushion, ball 1 is generally left above ball 3—a situation not so favourable as when

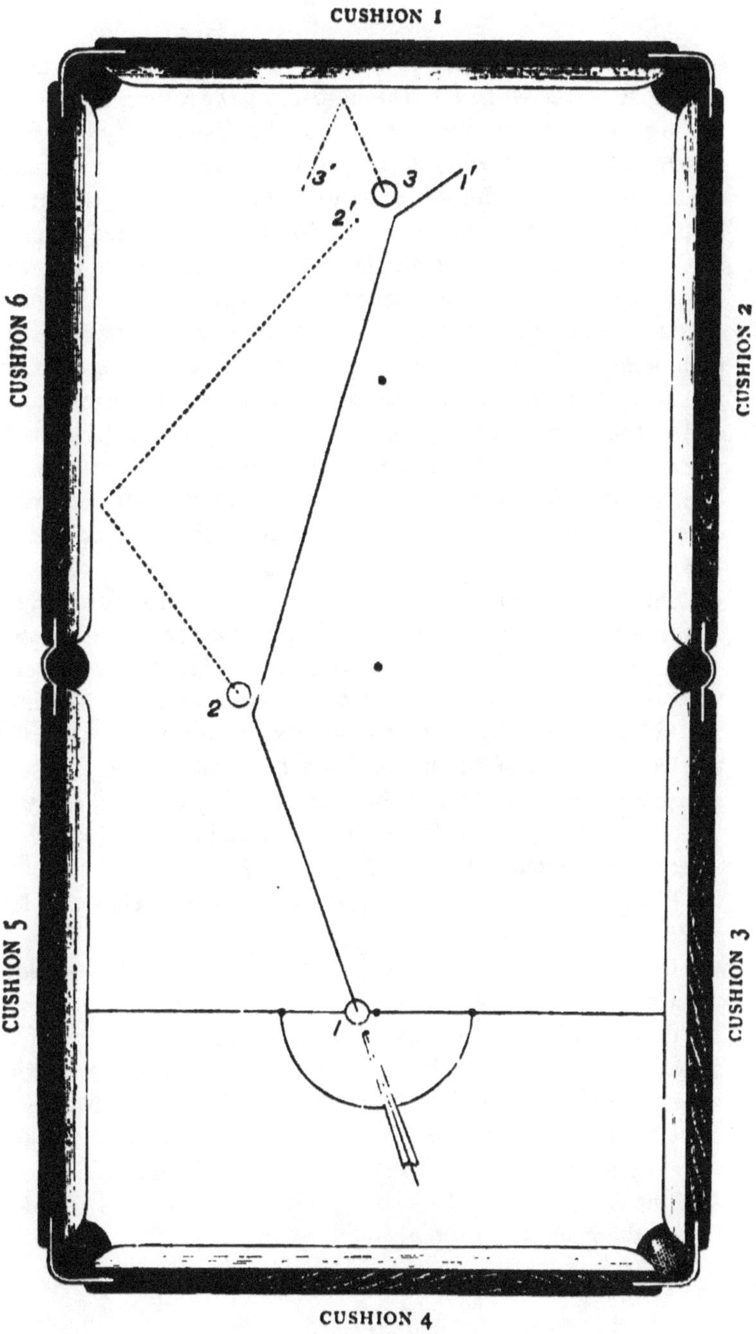
CUSHION 1
CUSHION 6
CUSHION 2
3'
3
1'
2'
2
CUSHION 5
CUSHION 3
1
CUSHION 4

Diagram XII.

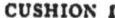

ball 1 is below the other two balls. It often happens, however, that ball 2 is so left that a losing hazard from it into the left top pocket can be made, and the break may be thus continued. The further it is desired to bring ball 2 towards the left top pocket, the more towards baulk centre should ball 1 be placed; and the nearer to the spot it may be wished to leave it, the finer should the stroke be set. One advantage of practising this stroke is that confidence is acquired in making the cannon from the cushion, which is in this instance greatly preferable to playing a forcing stroke direct, though many persons, thinking of the cannon alone, would erroneously select the latter mode of play. A substantial gain is made when the player has recognised that the stroke is almost exactly like the two just described, and that the top cushion may, save in a small extra allowance of strength, be completely ignored.

On Diagram XIV. two cannons are shown; to that marked A special attention is invited. The position, or a similar one, often occurs, and is as often incorrectly played by amateurs, when balls 2 and 3 are on the table, and 1 in hand. Thinking solely of making the cannon, the player usually spots 1 towards the right of the baulk for a half-ball stroke. Result, a cannon and separation of the balls, 2 being doubled towards baulk, 3 carried up the table and not improbably lodged in safety under cushion 6.

Place ball 2, 14 in. from cushion 5, 30 in. below the left middle pocket.

Ball 3, 11 in. from cushion 5, 17 in. below the left middle pocket.

Ball 1, 9 in. to the left of baulk centre. Play a gentle stroke on 2 so as to double it from the cushion to 3 and with strength sufficient for ball 1 to reach 3. The three balls will be left close together and not far from the left middle pocket. Care must be taken to prevent the balls being left in one straight line, and also to avoid a kiss between balls 1 and 2 before the cannon.

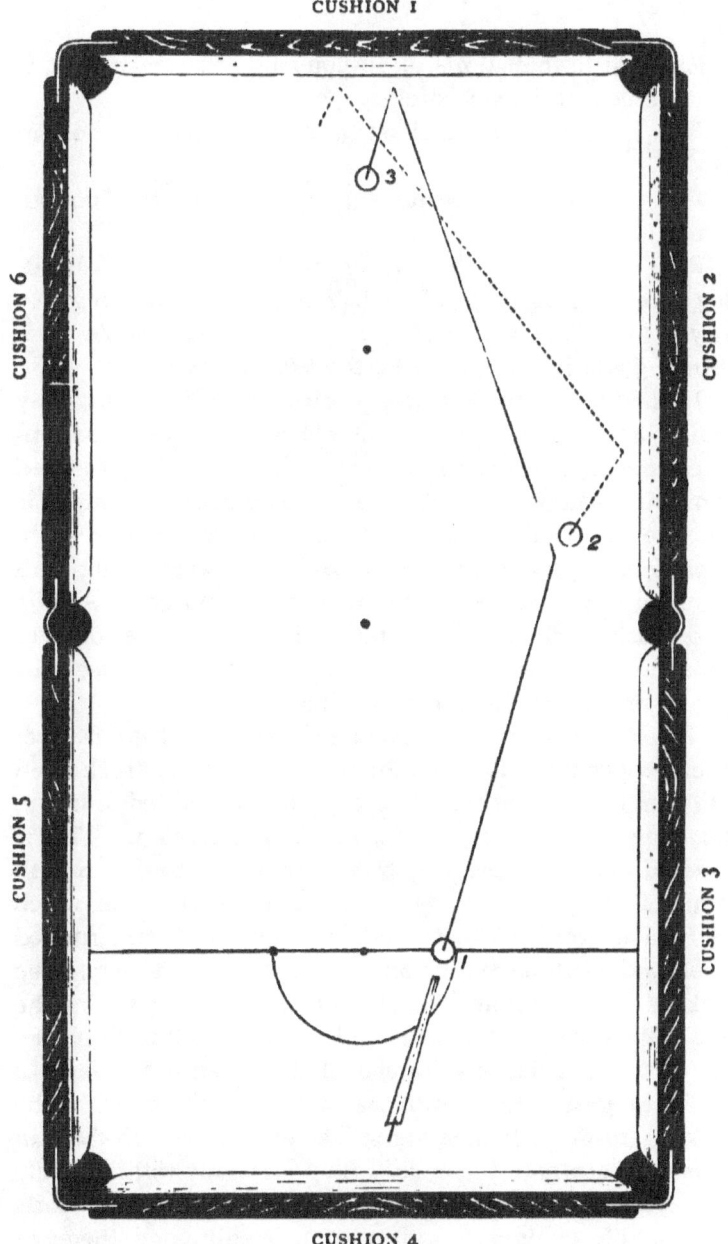

Diagram XIII.

Example B, though not of so common occurrence as A, is also an excellent practice stroke.

Ball 1, 5½ in. from cushion 3, 21½ in. from the bottom cushion.

Ball 2, 4 in. from cushion 3, 33 in. from the bottom cushion.

Ball 3, in front of the left top pocket, 3 or 4 in. from it. Play a centre ball stroke, about half-ball on 2, with strength to carry 1 to 3—say a free No. 1. Ball 2 will double from cushion 3 and join 1 and 3 near the left top pocket.

In this stroke accidents may happen, and if it be missed by a hair's breadth the adversary will rejoice. Ball 3 may be cannoned into the pocket and ball 2 may also go in; but, if played often, the result will generally be satisfactory and the stroke is therefore a fairly sound one. If ball 3 were the red, it would be prudent to play so as to leave ball 2 somewhat behind and thus reduce the danger of losing it in the pocket. A little consideration will show that the varieties of this stroke are numerous, and that by means of some of them the three balls may be brought to the top of the table.

The strokes shown in Diagram XV. exemplify that most useful class of cannons in which the velocity of ball 1, struck often with considerable force, is almost wholly transmitted to ball 2, and 1 retains little more than is required to reach 3. This is achieved in the first place by playing as full as the cannon will admit of on 2, and next by a peculiar use of the cue, which the French term *arrêté* because it is grasped and not permitted to follow the ball more than an inch or two after delivery. The stroke is a stab, and its intensity can be varied by raising the butt of the cue. The point of ball 1 to be struck is, as before, the centre, but delivery instead of being horizontal is at a smaller or greater angle with the surface of the table. The stroke is made as though the striker desired to stab the ball through its centre to the table. It springs away with more life than can be communicated by a horizontal stroke, and parts with that life on impact with 2 more readily, and therefore

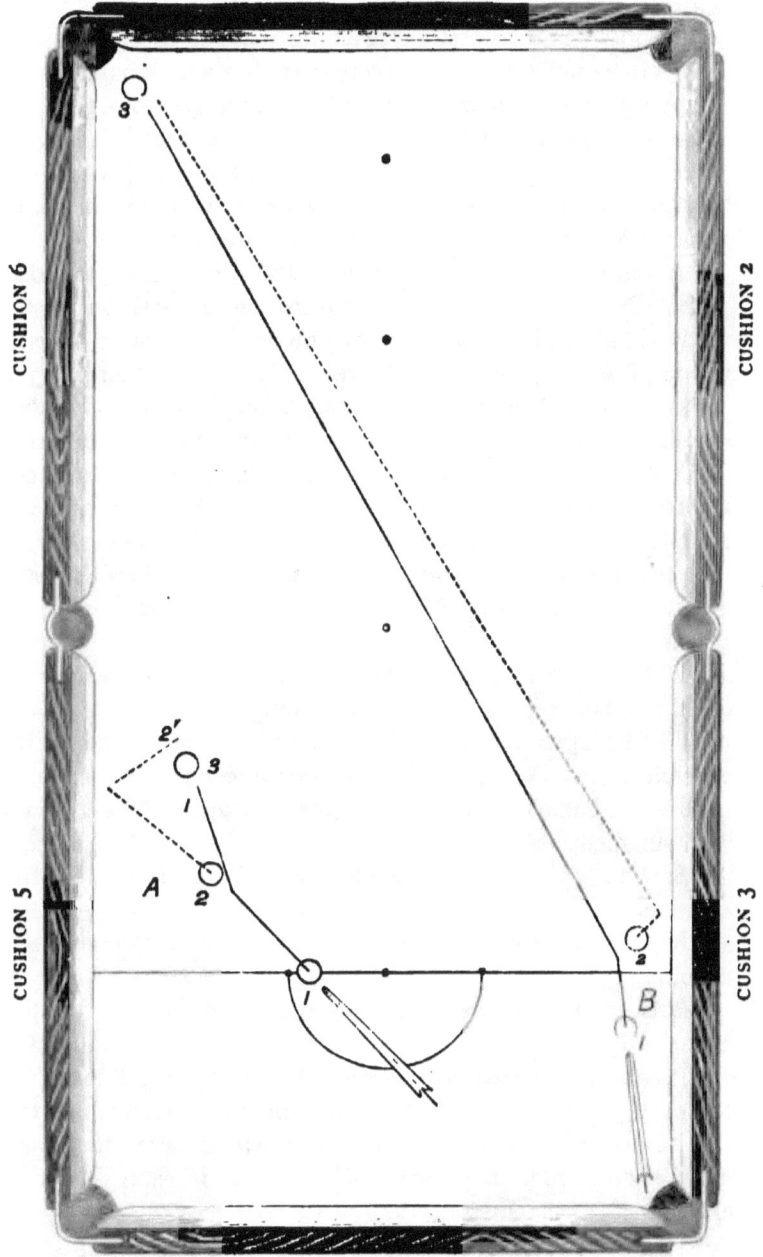

Diagram XIV.

expires or comes to rest on reaching 3 with greater certainty. The stab is not required in every case, but where ball 2 has a long path to travel and ball 3 is at a right angle from 2 or less, it cannot be dispensed with. Classified as a stroke, it may be placed between the horizontal centre and the screw, which will be described in the next chapter, whereby ball 1 is made to return towards the point of the cue after impact with 2.

A simple form of these cannons is shown at A on this diagram. No measurements are required, as the position is perfectly simple and equally good for practice when varied according to pleasure. It can be conveniently played when ball 3 is on the pyramid spot, ball 2 about 6 in. from it and rather nearer the player, ball 1 being between the player and 2 near the latter as shown. Play ball 1 nearly full on 2 with strength sufficient to cause its return from the cushion to 3, which 1 should reach but scarcely move. When played as shown across the table the stroke is always a gentle one, and when the balls are close to the cushion from which 2 has to return it must be played very softly indeed. The usual faults made in playing are that 2 is struck too hard and too fine, the result being that the three balls separate instead of coming together.

For B, a pretty little stroke useful in turning the corner at the left top pocket, the following measurements will help in placing the balls, which can however be set up from the diagram with sufficient accuracy.

Ball 1, $5\frac{1}{2}$ in. from cushion 6, $22\frac{1}{2}$ in. from the top cushion.

Ball 2, $3\frac{1}{2}$ in. (full) from cushion 6, $16\frac{1}{2}$ in. from the top cushion.

Ball 3, $8\frac{1}{2}$ in. from cushion 6, 13 in. from the top cushion.

Play a gentle stroke on 2 from $\frac{3}{4}$ to $\frac{1}{2}$ to the right so as just to reach 3 ; 2 will return from side and top cushions, and the three balls will be left together. It is evident that this stroke may be adapted to any corner of the table, an exercise which may be left to the student.

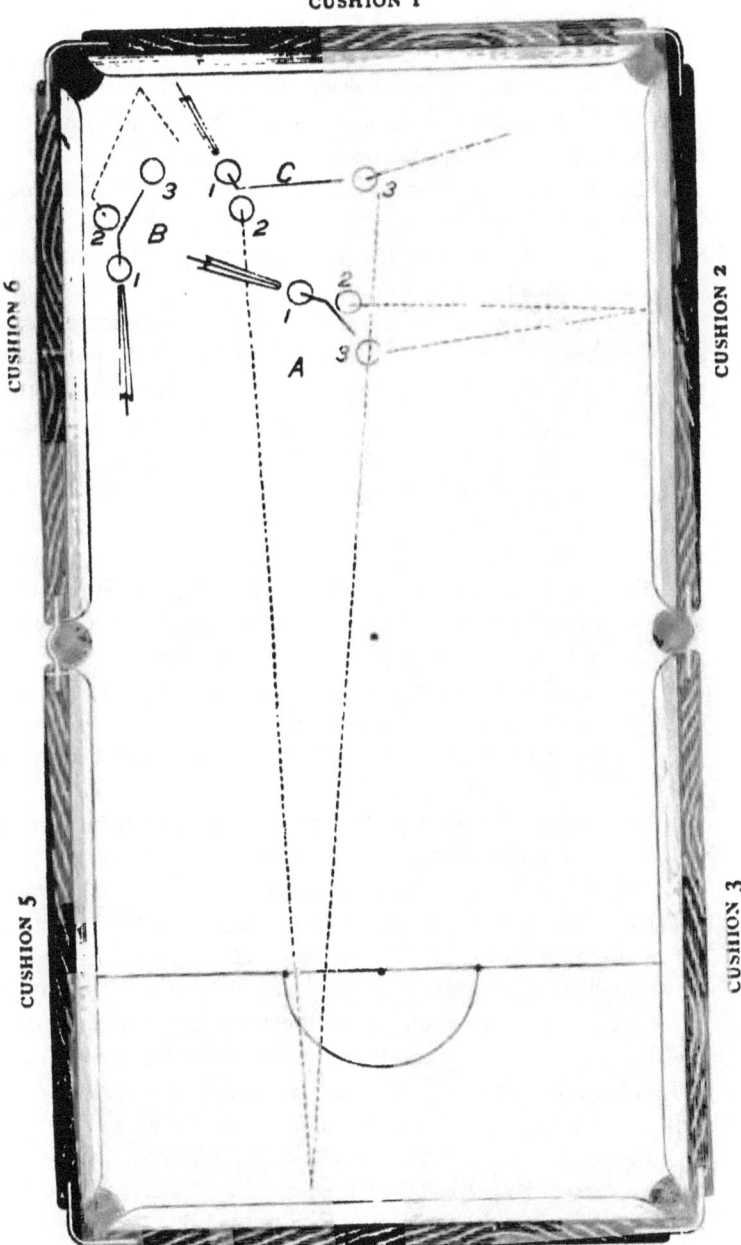

Diagram XV.

Example C.

Ball 2, 19 in. from cushion 6, 16½ in. from the top cushion; ball 3 on the spot; ball 1, 18 in. from cushion 6 and 12 in. from the top cushion.

Play a little less than full on 2 with strength to bring it back from the bottom cushion to the neighbourhood of the spot; ball 1 to travel to 3, which it moves slowly towards the right top corner pocket.

This stroke as exhibited at C is not very difficult, though some moderate execution is required, and an intelligent application of the stab will give more perfect control of the balls. As ball 3 is placed further from 2 and nearer the top cushion, so does the stroke require greater skill and judgment, the stab then becoming more necessary, as the energy or life of ball 1 must expire about the moment it reaches 3, otherwise the success of the stroke is much endangered.

Diagram XVI. shows a position of the balls which at first sight is apt to be regarded with dissatisfaction by the player.

Ball 2 is too near cushion 2 and too far from the right top pocket for a certain losing hazard; say 28 or 29 in. from top cushion and 5½ in. from the side.

Ball 3 is 3 in. from cushion 6 and 12 in. above the middle pocket.

Ball 1 is in the central line of the table, from 9 to 13 in. below the pyramid spot.

Play No. 1 strength finer than half-ball on 2, which strikes cushion 2 and travels towards ball 3; ball 1 makes the cannon off cushions 2 and 1, and sometimes off cushion 6 as well.

The danger of this stroke is that balls 1 and 2 may kiss just before ball 3 is reached, the result being disappointment for the player and a good opening for the adversary. In the modern game, however, a man should look for success to skill and enterprise which, though not without risk, lead to rapid scoring, rather than to tactics of obstruction, so dear to the heart of respectable mediocrity. The results of this stroke will be found to vary considerably. Sometimes ball 3

CUSHION I
CUSHION 6
CUSHION 2
2
1
3
CUSHION 5
CUSHION 3
CUSHION 4

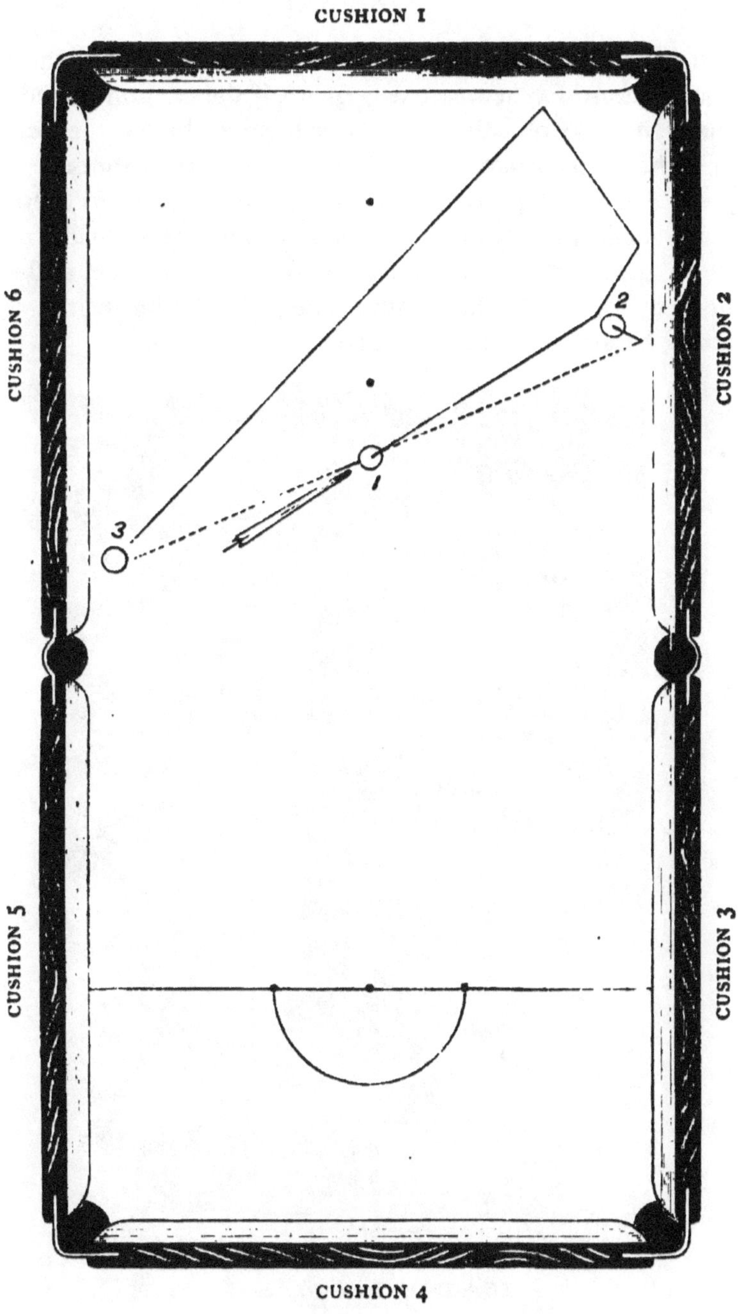

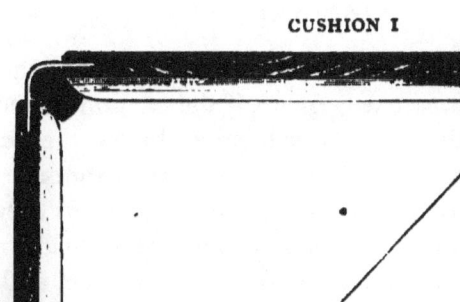

Diagram XVI.

will be placed over the left middle pocket with a winning or losing hazard for next stroke. Again, if the cannon is made on the right side of ball 3, ball 1 will travel below the pocket, and the next stroke will probably be another cannon. It is clear that this type of stroke can be modified at will; ball 1 may remain fixed whilst ball 3 is moved up the left side and 2 down the right side of the table, or ball 1 may be shifted a little up or down the central line; the limits being when losing hazards become preferable to the cannon.

High Bridge for a Cramped Stroke

www.ingramcontent.com/pod-product-compliance
Lightning Source LLC
Chambersburg PA
CBHW032006220426
43664CB00005B/162